PEOPLE AND THEIR ENVIRONMENT

Series editor: Neil Punnett

Agriculture and Industry

Neil Punnett

Oxford University Press

Pupil Profile Sheets

A Pupil Profile base sheet is provided which can be copied to provide sheets for each pupil. It is intended that each pupil should receive a profile sheet at the end of each Unit in this book.

At the end of each Unit is an Assessment. The second page of the Assessment contains a box in which the details for the Pupil Profile Sheets are listed. The teacher can transfer the details to the base sheet.

The profile will be completed following discussion between the teacher and pupil. It will therefore provide an agreed record of achievement throughout the course. It is hoped that the profile will help to enhance the learning of pupils, increase motivation, and provide diagnostic information for the teacher.

Contents

Unit 1 The agricultural system 4
1.1 Introduction 4
1.2 Choice of farming 6
1.3 A classification of agricultural systems 8
1.4 Agricultural land use patterns 10
Assessment 12

Unit 2 Agricultural regions 14
2.1 The Lake District 14
2.2 Farming in Norway 16
2.3 East Anglia 18
2.4 Farming in Denmark 20
2.5 Mediterranean farming 22
2.6 Factory farming 24
2.7 The Common Agricultural Policy 26
Assessment 28

Unit 3 Third World agriculture 30
3.1 Nomadic herders 30
3.2 Subsistence farming 32
3.3 Cash crops: plantations 34
3.4 Cash crops: cocoa 36
3.5 The big projects 38
3.6 An uncertain future 40
Assessment 42

Unit 4 The industrial system 44
4.1 Introduction 44
4.2 Industry as a system 46
4.3 Industrial location 1 48
4.4 Industrial location 2 50
Assessment 52

Unit 5 Key industries 54
5.1 Oil refining 54
5.2 The steel industry 1 56
5.3 The steel industry 2 58
5.4 The motor industry 60
5.5 A vehicle factory 62
5.6 The defence industry 64
5.7 High-tech industry 66
5.8 Offices 68
5.9 Retailing 70
Assessment 72

Unit 6 Industrial regions 74
6.1 South Wales 1 74
6.2 South Wales 2 76
6.3 The port industries of Rotterdam 78
6.4 The Randstad 80
6.5 The Western Corridor 82
6.6 Why not move to the centre of London? 84
Assessment 86

Unit 7 Third World industry 88
7.1 The importance of industry 88
7.2 Heavy industry in India 90
7.3 Brazilian motor industry 92
7.4 The newly industrialized countries 94
7.5 Made in Korea 96
7.6 Is industry the answer? 98
Assessment 100

Unit 8 Selling Swindon by the pound 102
8.1 Swindon's early growth 102
8.2 The fastest growing town in Western Europe 104
8.3 The industry of the future? 106
Assessment 108

Unit 9 Post-industrial Britain 110
9.1 The geography of unemployment 110
9.2 Government aid 112
9.3 The EC regional policy 114
9.4 The leisure boom 116
9.5 Leisure in the countryside 118
9.6 The Brecon Beacons National Park 120
Assessment 122

Index 125

Acknowledgements 126

Photocopiable Pupil Profile base sheet 128

1.1 Introduction

Unit 1: The agricultural system

The shelves of a superstore are stacked high with food. In the store shown in Figure A we can see:

milk from England
lamb from New Zealand
cans of tuna fish from the Philippines
cucumbers from the Netherlands
tomatoes from Italy
oranges from Spain
mangoes from Jamaica
figs from Turkey
dates from Tunisia
canned beef from Botswana
tea from Sri Lanka
coffee from Brazil
wine from Yugoslavia
apples from France
chocolates from Switzerland
passion fruit from Kenya
grapes from Israel
pineapples from the Ivory Coast
grapefruit from the USA
potatoes from Egypt
walnuts from China
curry powder from India
bananas from Colombia
cocoa from Ghana
sausage from West Germany
jam from Hungary

Figure A *(right)* Food on sale in a superstore

All this food is produced by farmers. They live in many different countries throughout the world and work on many different types of farm, but they have much in common with each other. Each farmer can view his or her farm as a *system* with inputs and outputs (Figure B). The inputs of a farm include the soil, the climate, the relief (shape and form of the land), the seed, plants, animals and the workforce. The farmer carries out a number of processes which may include ploughing, sowing and harvesting. These result in the outputs of the farm which include crops, meat and milk. The outputs will then be sent to the market.

Figure B The farm as a system

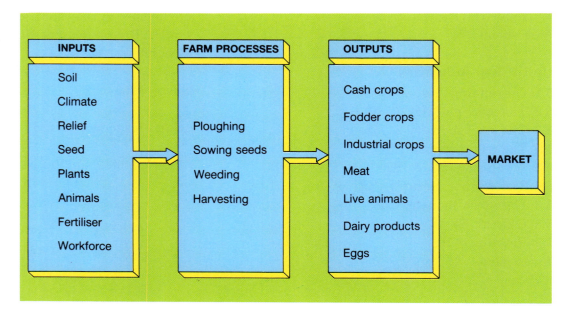

Figure C Four farms: Spain (*above left*), Kashmir (*above*), Argentina (*left*), Canada (*below left*)

QUESTIONS

1 Study the list of products in the superstore given in the text.
   a) Which product is the odd one out?
   b) On an outline map of the world shade in each of the countries listed.
   c) Name one large country whose farm products are not included in the list. Try to explain why.
   d) On your next visit to a large supermarket make your own list of the countries whose products are for sale.

2 Figure C shows four farms. Describe the scene in each photograph.

3 a) Copy the diagram below which is an incomplete version of a farm shown as a system. Print the words OUTPUT, MARKET and INPUT in the correct box.

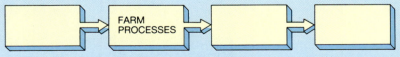

b) Give three examples of each of inputs, processes and outputs in a farm system.

1.2 Choice of farming

The photographs (Figures A and B) show two very different types of farm. The farm in Figure A concentrates on sheep while that in Figure B grows a range of crops. The sheep farm is in the Lake District, the arable farm is in Norfolk. What affects the choice of farming? Answer questions 1 and 2 before reading on.

Relief and climate will affect farming. Also important will be the soils. How deep are they? What plant *nutrients* do they contain? Do they allow water to drain through them, or are they often waterlogged? In the Lake District soils are generally thin and acid, containing few plant nutrients. Many of the soils are poorly drained and peaty. In East Anglia there is a rich variety of soils. Chalk, silts and sands have been largely covered by boulder clay deposited by ice sheets during the Ice Age.

The farmer's decision will be affected by factors apart from the physical geography of the area:

Money. The richer the farmer the more that can be spent upon the farm to improve it. New techniques, machinery and chemicals can be used on the farm.

Labour. Some types of farming need more workers than others. A hill sheep farm may be run by only one person, plus several sheep dogs. A large arable farm in East Anglia may still need many workers despite the growth in machinery.

Figure A

Figure B

Figure C The farming system of a Lake District hill farm

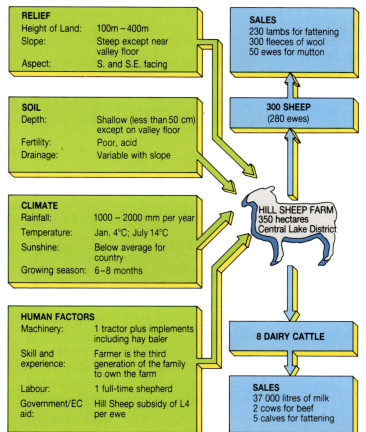

Figure D The farming system of an East Anglian arable farm

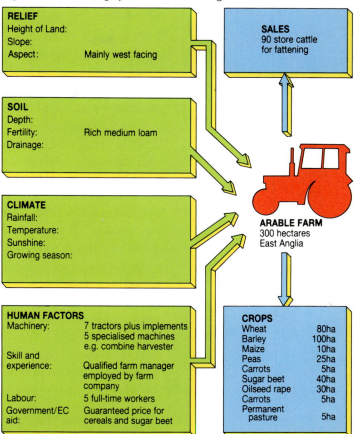

Contracts. If the farmer can get a contract for a food processing company, such as a freezing or canning firm, he or she will have an assured source of income.

Interests. A farmer will follow his or her interests in farming.

Government and EC policy. Farming policies provide grants, loans, tax relief, guaranteed prices and subsidies which can provide a vital source of income to farmers.

The final choice of farming will depend upon how much research and knowledge the farmer has. The farmer's *perception* of the conditions may not be correct. Wrong choices can be made. Often a farmer may choose a type of farming simply because that is what other farmers in the area practise. A famous example is provided by the farmers of Romney Marsh in Kent who raised sheep until a newcomer showed that more money could be made from growing vegetables and cereals.

QUESTIONS

1 a) Describe the landscape in the two photographs.
  b) How does the landscape affect the type of farming possible?

2 Find the maps showing the climate of Britain in your atlas.
  a) What are the January and July temperatures in (i) the central Lake District (ii) west Norfolk?
  b) How does temperature affect the type of farming possible?
  c) What is the average annual rainfall in the central Lake District and west Norfolk?
  d) How do rainfall totals affect the type of farming possible?

3 How can the type of soil affect farming?

4 Figure C shows the farm system of the Lake District hill farm shown in Figure A.
  a) Study the diagram carefully. Copy Figure D and complete it to show conditions favourable to arable farming in East Anglia.
  b) Draw a bar graph to illustrate the crops grown on the East Anglian farm.
  c) How might each of the following crops be marketed or used on the East Anglian farm: (i) barley (ii) peas (iii) carrots (iv) sugar beet (v) maize?
  d) Why are no arable crops grown on the Lake District farm?

5 a) Discuss the physical and economic factors which affect a farmer's decision on what to produce.
  b) What other factors influence a farmer's decision?

1.3 A classification of agricultural systems

Different types of farm can be classified into a number of *systems*.

1 The most basic division is between pastoral and arable. Pastoral farms raise livestock, arable farms grow crops. Of course, many farms do both; such farms are often called mixed farms.

2 The system of farming may be intensive or extensive. Intensive farming spends much money and time on the land to produce high *yields*, usually with highly mechanized and modern methods. Extensive farming uses small amounts of money and labour on large areas of land for low yields.

3 Many farmers, especially in the developing world, practise subsistence agriculture. This means that the farmers grow food mainly to feed themselves and their families. The most basic type of subsistence farming is shifting cultivation. Farmers make a clearing in the forest or savanna and grow crops for a

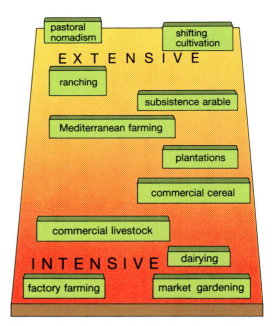

Figure A The intensity of various farming systems

number of years. They move on and make another clearing when the soil is exhausted and yields are low. Farmers who roam large areas in search of grazing for their livestock are called pastoral nomads. They have no permanent home. There are settled subsistence farmers too. As much as a quarter of the world's population is supported by subsistence rice farming in Asia. Other Asian, African and South American farmers grow a range of subsistence cereals and vegetables.

4 Commercial farmers grow crops for sale. Their livelihood depends upon their success and the price they get in the market for their produce. There are several commercial farming systems:

a) Plantations are large farms, mainly in the developing world, which concentrate on a single crop, like sugar, rubber, tea, coffee or palm oil.

b) Commercial cereal farming often concentrates on the production of a single crop: wheat, barley or maize. The prairies of North America, the steppes of the USSR and the pampas of Argentina are the major areas. The climate is dry (under 500 mm of rain per year) with hot summers and cool winters. These farms are very large and highly mechanized.

Figure B Growing tomatoes in a huge glasshouse

Figure C Planting rice

c) Mediterranean farming involves the growing of olives, vines and citrus fruit. Wheat is also grown. Wheat can grow through the wet winters and be harvested before the very hot and dry summers.

d) Fruit and vegetables are grown over large areas of North America, the Mediterranean lands, South Africa and Australia. They need many workers.

e) Market gardening is a form of fruit and vegetable farming that is concentrated on small farms around major urban areas. Much of the production may be in greenhouses.

f) Ranching involves the rearing of sheep and cattle for meat on the dry grasslands of North America, South America, South Africa, Australia and New Zealand. Animals roam freely over vast rough grazing areas and are rounded up at intervals for dipping, shearing or slaughter.

g) Dairy farming involves the production of milk, butter, cheese and yoghurt. It is concentrated in cool, moist climates where grass grows well. North-West Europe, northern USA, southern Australia and the North Island of New Zealand are the main areas. Dairy products are expensive and so rarely seen in poorer countries.

Land ownership

Ownership of agricultural land varies:

a) The farmer may own the land or rent it from a landowner.

b) Land may be divided into large estates owned by landowners who rent land to tenant farmers or employ low paid labourers to work the farm.

c) The land may be owned by a number of people who run it on a *co-operative basis*.

d) The land may be owned by the government. In many communist countries large privately-owned estates were taken over by the state. In the USSR state *collective* farms are run by farmworkers who either receive a wage from the government or keep part of their produce.

Figure D A hill sheep farm

Figure E Next week's bacon

QUESTIONS

1 What are (i) pastoral and (ii) arable farms?

2 'At Manor Farm much money and time is spent on the land to produce high crop yields. Maximum use is made of machines, chemical fertilisers and pesticides.' Is Manor Farm an intensive or extensive farm? Give reasons for your answer.

3 Explain what you understand by the following terms:
  a) subsistence farming
  b) shifting cultivation
  c) pastoral nomads
  d) commercial farming

4 Make a table listing the main types of commercial farming. Include a sentence describing each type.

5 Study the four farms shown in Figures B to E.
  a) Are they arable or pastoral farms?
  b) Are they intensive or extensive?
  c) What type of farm system do you think each farm involves?

1.4 Agricultural land use patterns

Whatever type of farming is practised, there are certain economic factors which affect the farmer. For example, distance affects all farmers. For the commercial farmer the time taken to travel from the farmhouse to the fields is time wasted since no money is being earned. For the subsistence farmer the time taken to travel from the farmhouse to the fields is also time wasted since it could have been spent on other things. All farmers will try to save themselves time by reducing the distances they have to travel. Of course, they may be prepared to travel further if there is the chance of using better soils, but this will result in higher yields which will overcome the costs of distance.

Some types of farming need more time spent on them than others. One way of measuring this is the Standard Man Day (SMD). This is a measure of the number of working days per year that a farm animal or crop needs.

Because distance is money to the farmer those crops or animals which require most attention will be located as close to the farmhouse as possible. For example, a fruit grower will have strawberries near the farmhouse and orchards further away; a cattle farmer will have dairy cows near the farmhouse and beef cows further away.

Figure B Examples of SMDs

SMDs per hectare		SMDs per head	
Grass	5	Sheep	2
Cereals	7	Pigs	3
Sugar Beet	43	Beef cattle	12
Potatoes	50	Dairy cows	36
Orchards	62		
Strawberries	111		

The Von Thunen model of agricultural land use

A German farmer, Von Thunen, proposed a model for the type of farming found around a town. He said that if the relief and climate of the area were the same, economic factors would decide the type of farming. A series of concentric circles would be seen with the most intensive farming near the city and

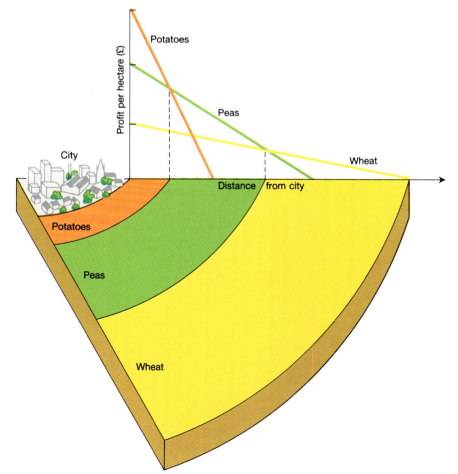

Figure A Economic rent and agricultural land use

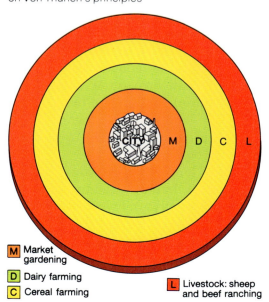

Figure C Land use around a European city based on Von Thunen's principles

M Market gardening
D Dairy farming
C Cereal farming
L Livestock: sheep and beef ranching

Figure D Land use on the urban fringe – fruit and vegetable growing near Tel Aviv

more extensive farming further away.

The principle of *economic rent* underlies the theory: different crops give different profits per hectare, varying with distance from the town because of the cost of transport. The graph (Figure A) shows that potatoes produce the highest yields per hectare and thus the highest profit, but they are very expensive to transport. If potatoes are grown a long way from the town the profit will be greatly cut by the higher costs of transport. At a certain distance away from the town the farmer will begin to make more profit from another crop which is cheaper to transport than potatoes, such as peas.

Von Thunen's model was first proposed as long ago as 1826 and it has clearly been overtaken by the pace of technological change in farming and transport. However, the concentric rings of land use can still be seen in general terms. It has been pointed out that much of the farmland on the edge of towns is in fact not used intensively any more. Instead there may be overgrown, untended meadows or grazing for horses. This is often because the land has been bought by people who are waiting for the best moment to sell it for building purposes.

QUESTIONS

1 a) How does distance affect commercial and subsistence farmers?
   b) Why might farmers be prepared to travel further?

2 The map below represents the fields of a large farm. The table gives the labour needs, in Standard Man Days per hectare, of the five main crops grown on the farm. Copy the map of the farm and show the most likely crops grown in each of the fields.

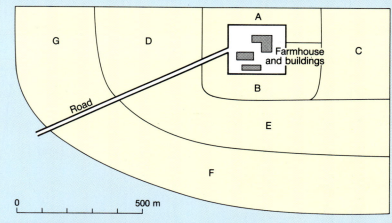

Labour needs of five crops

Crop	SMDs per ha	Farm area needed (ha)
Turnips	30	12
Wheat	7	85
Orchards	62	7
Grass	5	10
Potatoes	50	8

3 What do you understand by the principle of economic rent?

4 a) Explain the pattern of land use shown on Figure C.
   b) How might von Thunen's model be criticised today?

Unit 1 ASSESSMENT

1 What is the most likely type of farming in a mountainous area of Britain?
   A. shifting cultivation
   B. market gardening
   C. sheep rearing
   D. pig rearing
   E. cereal farming
   (1 mark)

2 Complete the systems diagram below for a farm by stating 3 main inputs, 3 main processes and 3 main outputs. (3 marks)

Main inputs	Main processes	Main outputs
1	1	1
2	2	2
3	3	3

Map A

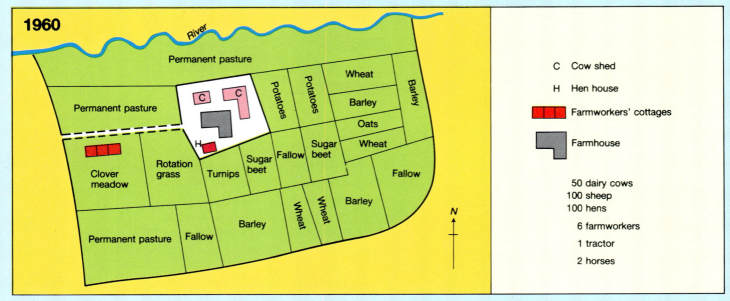

Map B

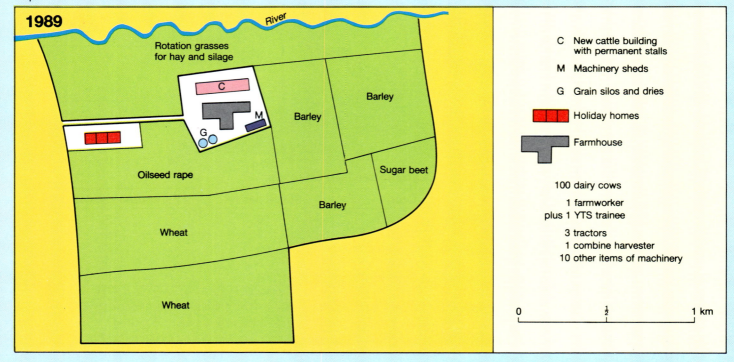

3 Explain why you would expect to find market gardening near a city and wheat farming further away (5 marks)

Study Maps A and B which show changes in a farm in eastern England. The following questions refer to the maps:

4 The farm is a mixed farm. Explain this term. (2 marks)

5 a) How has the livestock kept on the farm changed? (2 marks)
   b) Why do you think these changes have happened? (4 marks)

6 a) How many types of crop were grown in 1960? (1 mark)
   b) How many types of crop were grown in 1989? (1 mark)
   c) Which crop has been introduced onto the farm since 1960? (1 mark)
   d) Give two uses of this crop. (2 marks)

7 Explain why the variety of crops grown on the farm has been greatly reduced since 1960. (6 marks)

8 a) Describe the changes that have occurred in the number and size of the fields. (2 marks)
   b) Why do you think these changes have occurred? (4 marks)

9 a) Describe the changes that have occurred in the farm buildings and farmworkers' cottages. (3 marks)
   b) Why have these changes occurred? (6 marks)

10 a) Describe the changes that have occurred in the farm workforce. (2 marks)
   b) Why have these changes occurred? (4 marks)

11 Imagine that you are a young farmer trying to convince your bank manager of the need for progress on your farm. Write a letter to your bank manager listing the arguments in support of new farming methods. (10 marks)

12 The farm shown in the maps has seen many changes. Not everybody would think that these changes are a good thing. Choose three of the changes which have occurred and say why some people might oppose them. (9 marks)

TOTAL: 70 marks

Details for pupil profile sheet Unit 1

Knowledge and understanding

1 System
2 Input, Process, Output
3 Pastoral, arable farming
4 Intensive, extensive farming
5 Subsistence, commercial farming
6 Shifting cultivation
7 Plantation farming
8 Economic rent
9 Standard Man Day
10 Von Thunen's Model of agricultural land use

Skills

1 Complete a simple farm system diagram
2 Complete a complex farm system diagram
3 Use an atlas to find countries
4 Mark countries on an outline map using an atlas
5 Written description from a photograph
6 Reading climatic graphs from an atlas
7 Drawing a bar graph
8 Presenting textual information in the form of a table
9 Interpret change over time from maps

Values

1 Understand the role of decision-making in farm land use
2 Understand the role of perception of decision-makers
3 Awareness of contrasting attitudes to progress

2.1 The Welsh hill farm

Unit 2: Agricultural regions

Figure B shows the valley of the Afon Llia river in the Brecon Beacons National Park, South Wales. The beauty of this area attracts hundreds of thousands of tourists every year. Hills and mountains rise to over 800 metres. Countless streams flow seawards from the high land, following valleys once deepened and widened by Ice Age glaciers.

The Welsh mountains – an excellent place for a holiday, but not so easy to farm. The farmers in the Afon Llia Valley face the following:

- Rainfall of over 2000 mm per year.
- Low temperatures: cool summers (July average 14°C), cold winters (January average 3°C), low sunshine totals.
- Thin, infertile, acidic soils over much of the area, with outcrops of bare rock and screes (loose rock fragments at the base of a slope).
- There are deeper soils in the valley bottoms but these may be flooded and remain waterlogged. They need liming to improve grass growth.
- Competition for land from foresters who want to plant coniferous plantations, from water authorities who want to flood valley floors by building reservoirs and from industry which wants to quarry the area's minerals.

Only the highest mountain land has a truly natural landscape. Below about 600 metres sheep graze the rough pasture. Sheep are strong and hardy animals that can survive the harsh winters and graze on pastures which would not support cattle. Much of the higher land in the Welsh mountains is unfenced common land. 'Common' does not mean open to everybody; only registered 'commoners' have rights for their animals to graze common land. The common land of the Afon Llia Valley has been used for centuries by farmers from many parts of Powys.

Below the common rough pasture lie the upland hill farms with fields enclosed by stone walls. Farmers here concentrate on rearing sheep, but also rear some beef cattle. Lambs are sent for fattening in lowlands such as the Vale of Usk and the Vale of Glamorgan. The ewes are usually only brought down to the valley farms for lambing, shearing and dipping. The farmhouses are sited on the valley floors where the climate is milder and access is easier. Most are strong stone buildings which may be several centuries old.

The hill farmer may own a tractor and a grass cutter to cut the grass of the valley fields for hay or silage as animal feed. Otherwise there is little farm machinery, and little labour is needed. Often the only permanent labour force is the farmer and his or her family, plus the essential sheep dogs. The costs of hill farming are low. Unfortunately, the profits are also low. There are two abandoned farmhouses in the valley of the Afon Llia which provide evidence of the struggle to make a living as a hill farmer.

Few hill farmers could now survive without financial aid from the government and from the EC. During the

Figure A The Afon Llia

Figure B The Afon Llia Valley, South Wales – good farming country?

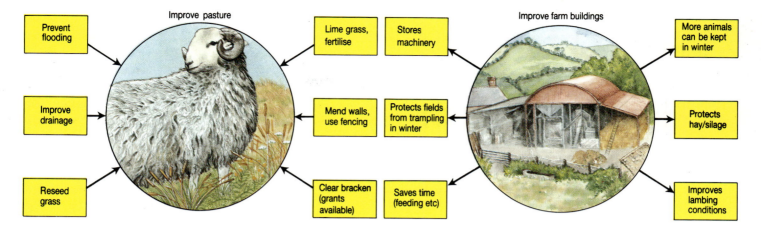

Figure C Improving hill farming

1970s prices for sheep fell by 50 per cent relative to industrial products; fodder and fuel costs rose steeply – many hill farmers were forced out of business or forced to find part-time work. Fortunately, 1980 saw the introduction of the 'sheepmeat regime' by the EC. This raised the guaranteed price for lamb by 25 per cent and made hill farming a safer living. Hill farmers now largely concentrate on sheep and beef cattle. The small dairy herds which many hill farmers used to keep have long gone; they cannot compete with the lowland dairy farmers.

Many improvements have been made to the hill farming system in recent years (Figure C). Nevertheless, most hill farmers seek extra money. They may earn it from forestry, part-time factory work or tourism. Bed and breakfast and farm holidays are provided by some hill farms. Many farmers hire out their land for camping and caravanning during the summer. Pony-trekking or riding stables attract many tourists.

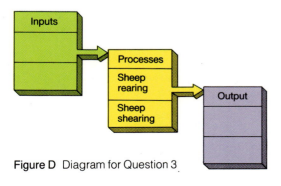

Figure D Diagram for Question 3

QUESTIONS

1 a) Where is the Brecon Beacons National Park?
   b) Using Figures A and B to help you, describe the landscape of the Brecon Beacons.

2 Copy out and complete the table below:

Problems facing the farmers in the Afon Llia Valley

Factor	Problems associated with this factor
Rainfall	
Temperatures	
Soils	
Competition for land	

3 Copy the systems diagram below (Figure D) which shows the hill farm system. Fill in the empty boxes to show TWO likely inputs and TWO likely outputs.

4 Study the table below:

Agricultural land use in Wales and England

| Land use | Percentage of total land | |
	WALES	ENGLAND
Cereals	4	34
Fodder crops	1	1
Fruit & vegetables	0.1	2.5
Temporary grass	10	10
Other crops	0.4	5.5
Permanent grass	48	32
Rough grazing	34.5	12
Woodland	2	3
Total	100	100

   a) Draw two pie charts or divided bars to represent these statistics.
   b) How does the land use in Wales differ from that in England?
   c) Suggest reasons for the differences you noted in b).

5 a) From where may hill farmers receive financial aid?
   b) How does this aid affect hill farming?

15

2.2 Farming in Norway

The coast of Norway is one of the scenic wonders of the world (Figure D). Steep, sometimes vertical cliffs rise above thousands of deep blue inlets of the sea. The inlets are *fjords* formed when the sea level rose after the last Ice Age, drowning the deep glaciated valleys.

It is not surprising that this beautiful scenery is a major tourist attraction. The fjords of Norway may be ideal for a holiday, but they are not so easy to farm.

The fjordside farmers face the same problems as mountainside farmers elsewhere in Europe. But they have the added problem that many of the valley floors (which provide the best farmland in mountain regions) lie deep beneath the sea! The climate certainly doesn't help. This is one of the wettest areas of Europe with average annual rainfall well above 2000 mm. Mists and low cloud reduce the sunshine amounts. However, despite its northerly latitude, western Norway is not as cold as you might expect. An ocean current called the North Atlantic Drift brings warm water across the Atlantic Ocean from the Gulf of Mexico. This makes the climate milder and keeps the fjords free of ice. (January temperatures average 0°C or higher.)

The fjordside farms are small. Most are less than 10 hectares in area. Maximum use is made of every scrap of flat land. Rivers have helped the farmers since they carry sediment which they deposit when entering the still waters of the fjord. Over the centuries the sediment forms *deltaic flats* at the head of the fjord or where tributaries or waterfalls enter it. Raised beaches (strandflat) marking earlier, higher sea levels also provide flat land.

The fjordside farms obtain their main income from dairy cattle. The main

Figure A The fjordside farm

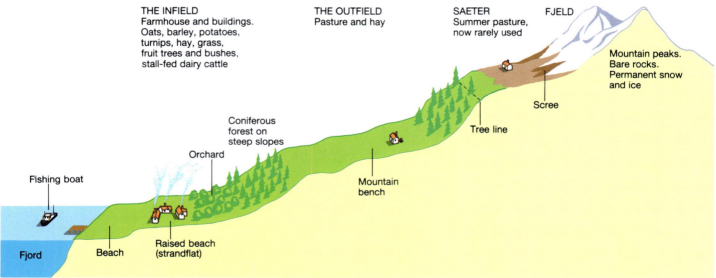

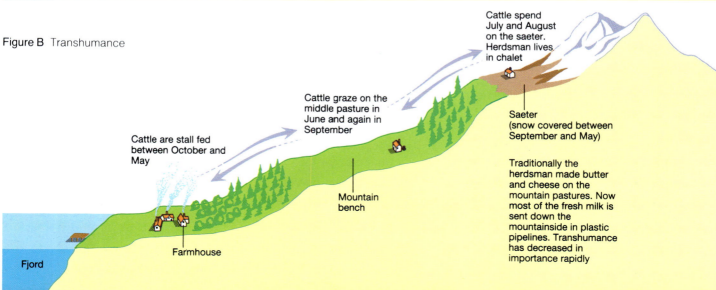

Figure B Transhumance

Figure C Picking raspberries beside Sogne Fjord

crops grown are grass for hay, oats, barley and potatoes for fodder. The cattle are kept in their stalls for much of the year and are fed on the fodder and commercial feedstuffs. The rapid population increase of several towns in western Norway due to North Sea oil and gas operations has increased the demand for fresh milk. In remoter areas most of the milk is turned into less perishable products such as cheese, butter, and yoghurt. In the past *transhumance* (Figure B) was common, but it is a difficult practice and the use of chemical fertilisers to raise the yields of the infield pastures plus the increased use of commercial feedstuffs has made transhumance rare today.

In the more southerly fjords some farmers have specialized in the production of vegetables and fruit. Summer's long hours of daylight help this form of farming. Strawberries, raspberries, tomatoes and cucumbers are grown in glasshouses or polythene 'tunnels' on south-facing slopes. Orchards of apples, pears, plums and cherries have been introduced on well-drained slopes.

The fjordside farms are usually run by a single family. Fjordside farming is hard work, and there is not much money to be made. Traditionally the farmers have gained extra money from fishing and forestry. Tourism offers new sources of income, from carving and selling wooden souvenirs to hiring out land for campers. Many farmers now work in the oil industry and run their farms on a part-time basis. The Norwegian government has been alarmed by the numbers of farms closing. Since 1975 it has followed a price guarantee policy which gives farmers a similar income to factory workers. This is paid for partly by Norway's oil money, but also partly by the high prices passed on to the customer.

Figure D The QE2 is dwarfed by the sheer cliffs of a fjord

QUESTIONS

1 a) Describe the landscape shown in the photograph above.
   b) What problems will the relief of this area pose to farmers?
   c) What is the climate of this area and what problems will this pose to farmers?

2 What are deltaic flats and why are they important to fjordside farmers?

3 Name (i) two cereal crops (ii) two roots crops and (iii) two fruits which are grown on fjordside farms and suggest uses of the crops.

4 Explain the following terms:
   (i) fjord (ii) saeter (iii) fjeld (iv) strandflat.

5 a) What is transhumance?
   b) Why is transhumance declining?

6 a) Name four ways by which fjordside farmers may earn extra income.
   b) Why is it necessary for the farmers to earn extra income?

7 What effects have Norway's North Sea oil and gas developments had upon fjordside farming?

8 a) What has the Norwegian government done to protect fjordside farmers?
   b) Why does the government feel that this is necessary?

2.3 East Anglia

Giant combine harvesters are at work on a huge field of wheat. This is part of the 'English prairies', so called because the landscape is similar to that of the prairies of Canada. The traditional small English fields with their high hedgerows are a thing of the past in East Anglia. The farmers have 'grubbed up' the hedges in order to give their machines longer runs without turning. Why is this area the granary of England? The following physical factors help to explain:

Relief. The central belt of East Anglia is flat or gently rolling country. This makes it very suitable for the use of machinery.

Soils. The soils are chalky boulder clay, deep and rich in plant nutrients. The boulder clay has been left by ice sheets which covered the area during the Ice Age.

Climate. This is the driest part of Britain with a total rainfall of under 650 mm a year over much of the region. Much of the rain falls during the growing season when it is most needed. The summers are warm with a daytime average of over 21°C in July and sunny (over 6.5 hours of sunshine per day in July). The cold winters (average 3°C in January) have hard frosts which help to kill diseases and break up the soil to assist ploughing.

Figure A

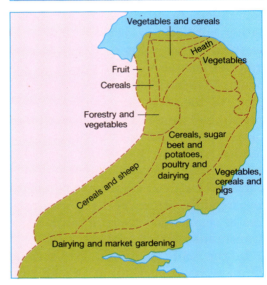

Figure B The top map shows soil types, the lower map shows farming regions

There are many human factors which also help to explain the success of arable farming in East Anglia. The farms are large and efficient, often over 200 hectares in area. The system of farming on such farms has been called 'agri-business'. Many of the farms are owned by companies and run by farm managers employed by the company. The companies have the money needed to invest in new farming methods. Much use is made of machines and chemicals. A typical agri-business might have the following machines: five tractors, two combine harvesters, muck spreaders, sprayers, ploughs, harrows, seed drills, trailers, and a grain drier.

The grain grown on such farms is used in the manufacture of cakes and biscuits. It may be mixed with 'hard' wheat from Canada and the USA for bread making. An increasingly important use for barley is as an animal feed.

In addition to wheat and barley, sugar beet and potatoes are also important in the chalky boulder clay area and there are pastures for dairy cattle on the heavier clay soils.

Elsewhere in East Anglia are areas specializing in fruit and vegetables. The Goodsands area of north Norfolk specializes in peas, carrots and cabbages. The sandy Breckland, used only for forestry until recently, has had its soils improved and carrots, parsnips and asparagus are grown. The loam soil area of north-east Norfolk now concentrates on peas and beans. The specialization is due to the development of *contract farming* in which a food company (such as Ross or Bird's Eye) agrees to purchase a crop from a farmer at a fixed price. The growth in home freezers has increased the demand for frozen vegetables.

Figure C High-technology on the farm

QUESTIONS

1. a) Where is East Anglia?
   b) Name three counties in East Anglia.
2. a) Describe the scene in Figure A.
   b) Why is this area called the 'English prairies'?
3. What does 'the granary of England' mean?
4. What is an 'agri-business'?
5. Study the table below:

Major land uses in East Anglia

Land use	Percentage of total area
Barley	32
Wheat	18
Permanent pasture	9
Vegetables	8
Sugar beet	8
Potatoes	6
Soft fruit	4
Oilseed rape	2
Other crops	2
Temporary grassland	8
Rough grazing	3

a) Draw a bar graph to illustrate the figures in the table.
b) What percentage of the total land use is taken up by cereal crops?
c) Why is East Anglia so suitable for growing cereal crops?

6. Complete the farming system diagram below for an 'agri-business' in East Anglia.

Large agri-business in Norfolk, 450 hectares, large open cereal fields

Inputs	Outputs
Human: Run by qualified farm manager, 4 full-time workers, owned by large London-based company, contract for barley from local brewery.	
Relief:	
Soils:	
Climate:	
Technology:	

2.4 Farming in Denmark

Food from Denmark is heavily advertised in Britain. Danish food fills shelves in our supermarkets. Denmark is one of the most efficient farming countries in the world. Yet the land of Denmark is not highly suited to farming. The soils of the country have been deposited by an ice sheet which flowed westwards across Denmark during the Ice Age.

As Figure B shows, eastern Jutland and the islands were covered by the ice sheet which deposited boulder clay. The boulder clay is moderately fertile, but it is heavy and poorly drained. The ice sheet stopped at the centre of Jutland, depositing a ridge of clay, stones and boulders called a terminal moraine. This is mainly infertile. In places the terminal moraine forms hills over 200 metres high. Meltwater streams flowed westwards from the terminal moraine. The streams deposited outwash sands and gravels over western Jutland. The outwash is infertile, supporting only heath and marshland under natural conditions.

Danish farmers have spent much time and money on improving the soils of their country. Fertilisers, lime and soil conditioners have transformed the land. Western Jutland is now under permanent pasture, oats and potatoes with coniferous forest in the sandier areas. Eastern Denmark is the main arable farming region, with wheat, barley, sugar beet, fruit and market gardening.

Before 1880 Danish farmers concentrated on wheat and barley. The opening up of the American West led to increasing supplies of grain from US and Canadian farms. The vast prairie farms could grow grain much more cheaply than the Danes. The competition threatened the Danish farmers' future. They had to take action to survive. Increased demand for dairy products from the growing industrial populations of the UK, Belgium and Germany led the Danes to turn to dairy farming.

The Danes developed a modern, scientific form of dairy farming which included:
- Selective breeding of animals developed the Danish Red cow which produces high milk yields from poor quality grass.
- The invention of a number of dairy machines such as the cream separator.
- The heavy use of fertiliser and farm machinery.
- Agricultural colleges to train farmers in the latest techniques.
- The development of co-operative associations (see Figure C).

Associated with the dairying is pig rearing since the pigs can be fed on the skimmed milk returned from the creameries. Selective breeding developed the Landrace pig whose long sides produce high quality bacon.

Today, pig and dairy products still make up 70 per cent of Danish farm incomes, but the farms themselves have changed greatly in recent years:
- The number of farms has fallen from 140000 in 1970 to 80000 by 1990.
- The average size of farms has increased from 21 hectares in 1970 to 46 hectares by 1990.
- The agricultural workforce fell from 200000 in 1970 to 85000 by 1990. This was due to increased mechanization

Figure A Some Danish food products sold in the UK

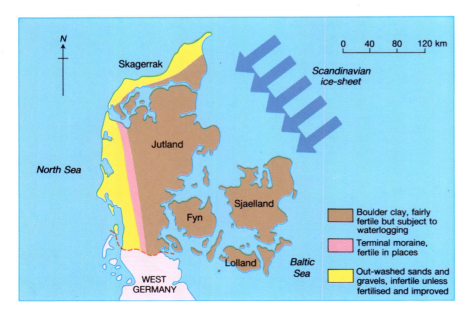

Figure B Denmark's glacial deposits and soil fertility

and the lure of higher paid jobs in industry.

- The dairy herd has fallen from 1.4 million in 1975 to 1.0 million in 1986. The decline is due to dairying's high labour demands and the drop in demand for butter as a result of competition from margarine and low fat vegetable spreads. This has caused an increase in pig farming (8 million pigs in 1975, 14 million in 1986) and in cereals (60 per cent of agricultural area in 1970, 77 per cent by 1986).

The modern Danish farm has the animals kept indoors all the time in hygienically controlled environments where they are fed on concentrated feedstuffs. The land is mainly used for the intensive production of fodder crops, especially barley. Even on those farms where the animals are still allowed to graze outdoors they are strictly controlled by the use of portable electric fences.

The markets for Danish farm products have changed since Denmark entered the EC in 1973. Danish exports of butter to Britain fell from 80 per cent of the total in 1970 to 50 per cent by 1986, and exports of ham and bacon to Britain fell from 60 per cent of the total in 1970 to 42 per cent by 1986. The Danes have found new markets within the EC and also further afield such as Japan and the USA. Thirty per cent of Danish butter and cheese exports are now to the Middle East.

Danish farming is supported by the skill of Danish agricultural scientists who have introduced and improved techniques and products. For example, in the 1970s they discovered a way to make feta cheese from cow's milk. Feta is usually made from sheep or goat's milk and is the main form of cheese eaten in the Middle East. Large export orders were won for the new cheese and by the mid-1980s cheese had overtaken butter as Denmark's major dairy export.

Figure C Co-operative farming in Denmark

Co-operatives operate in the following ways:
- Members can buy fertiliser, seed and feedstuffs in bulk, so saving money
- Purchase expensive farm machinery which individual farmers cannot afford
- Provide transport to collect milk and animals, and to take them to customers or processing factories
- Own and operate dairies, bacon-curing factories, slaughterhouses, egg – and poultry-packing plants, etc.
- Provide advisory services
- Set high standards for products – failure to meet the standards can lead to the rejection of a farmer's products
- Provide grants and loans

Danish farmers each belong to several co-operatives

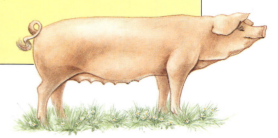

QUESTIONS

1. Name four Danish food products.
2. Copy Figure B and state briefly how the Ice Age has affected soils in Denmark.
3. How have Danish farmers improved the soils of their farms?
4. What did Danish farmers concentrate on before 1880 and why did they change to dairy farming after 1880?
5. What evidence is there that Danish farming is modern and scientific?
6. a) Describe briefly what a farming co-operative association is.
   b) What is the role of co-operative associations in Danish farming?
7. Study the table below:

The sources of income of Danish farmers

Source	Percentage of total income
Pigs	42
Dairy cattle	26
Beef cattle	18
Poultry	8
Others	6
Total	100

a) Draw a pie graph or divided bar graph to illustrate the statistics in the table.
b) List the three main sources of Danish farm income.
c) In what ways have the markets for exports of these products changed in recent years?

2.5 Mediterranean farming

The word 'Mediterranean' may make you think of long summer days lazing on a beach in Spain ... clear blue skies, a blazing hot sun and a deep blue sea. The countries around the Mediterranean Sea enjoy long, hot, dry summers. This attracts millions of tourists from the countries of northern Europe, whose summers are less reliable for holidays. Winter visitors may be disappointed, however. Although the temperature will be milder than northern Europe, the weather may well be dull, and wet (Figure A).

Month	J	F	M	A	M	J	J	A	S	O	N	D
Temperature (°C)	12	13	14	15	19	22	26	26	23	19	16	13
Rainfall (mm)	30	22	18	32	16	2	0	5	20	18	32	38

Figure A Climate statistics for Alicante, Spain

The climate poses problems for farmers in the Mediterranean region. The long summer drought, which attracts the tourists, makes farming difficult. In the past the farmers grew a few crops which could survive long dry periods, such as wheat, olives and vines, and kept hardy sheep and goats. This traditional style of farming continues in remoter and less developed areas of the Mediterranean region. But the long summer offers great potential for farming if only irrigation can be supplied.

Figure B Irrigated land on the Plain of Valencia

Figure C Heurtas of Spain

Spain is now the most irrigated country in Europe with over 3 million hectares of land served by irrigation systems (Figure C). On the narrow coastal plain, rivers provide water and light alluvial soils. The water is channelled to small, intensively cultivated fields called *huertas*. The huertas grow fruit, vegetables and salad crops.

Figure D shows the Plain of Valencia, an example of the large new irrigation schemes which have been built in southern Spain. Dams have been built in the mountainous valleys above the coastal plain. The reservoirs behind the dams hold back water during the winter and spring, preventing the serious flooding which used to occur in the valleys of the rivers Jucar and Turia. The dams also have small hydro-electric power stations. Concrete irrigation channels now carry the water from the rivers to fields which can grow oranges, lemons, potatoes and rice rather than wheat or olives.

Perhaps the most remarkable development in Mediterranean farming has occurred in the Almeria province of southern Spain. This province has been called 'the California of Europe'. The US state of California has a Mediterranean-style climate; large scale irrigation schemes have allowed the intensive production of fruit and vegetables. The same thing has happened in Almeria. Since 1970 the area around the town of El Eijido has been transformed into a landscape of plastic and polythene. Plastic greenhouses covering 12 000 hectares have been built (for comparison, there are only 2 200 hectares of greenhouses in the whole of the UK). Over 15 000 smallholder farmers own greenhouses. The average size of holding is only 0.75 hectares. Hundreds of thousands of tonnes of tomatoes, cucumbers, peppers, beans, cabbages, lettuce, melons and courgettes are grown in the hothouse atmosphere of the plastic greenhouses. The greenhouses are irrigated from deep wells tapping huge underground supplies of water. The crops are sent by lorry to the supermarkets of northern Europe. Over 200 000 tonnes, earning £200 million, were exported from Almeria in 1986.

The greenhouses have made El Eijido one of the most prosperous towns in Spain. Over 12 000 migrant workers add to the town's population of 36 000. The rapid development of the area has not been without problems, however:

- Many of the migrant workers are low paid and live in cramped and insanitary housing.
- Some of the water supplies have been contaminated with seawater because too much water has been extracted.
- The plastic greenhouses and irrigation systems are very expensive to build and maintain; the plastic is vulnerable to high winds and has to be replaced every two or three years.

Spain joined the EC in 1986. But it will be ten years before Spanish fruit and vegetables are allowed into the EC free of import duties. This was designed to protect EC growers, especially in France and the Netherlands. Spain's new breed of Mediterranean farmers will threaten these EC farmers.

Figure D The weird landscape of El Eijido seen from the air

QUESTIONS

1. Study the table showing the climate of Alicante.
   a) Draw a bar graph to illustrate the rainfall statistics and a line graph to represent the temperature statistics.
   b) What is the range of temperature?
   c) What is the total rainfall?
   d) What is the total rainfall of the three months (i) November, December and January (ii) June, July and August?
   e) What problems does this climate pose to the farmer?

2. What was the traditional system of farming developed in the Mediterranean region?

3. Describe the irrigation scheme in the Plain of Valencia.

4. Why is Almeria called 'the California of Europe'?

5. a) Describe the farming system of the fruit and vegetable growing area around El Eijido.
   b) How can the smallholders make a profit when the average size of their farms is only 0.75 hectares?
   c) What problems have been created by the greenhouse farming of El Eijido?

2.6 Factory farming

Until the 1960s chicken meat was a luxury for most British families. Chicken was as expensive as beef and pork. Within a few years, however, chicken had become the cheapest meat available in British shops. This change in prices was due to a change in farming methods.

The traditional method of raising chickens is called 'free range'. The chickens are allowed to roam around the farmyard. Corn is scattered at regular intervals for the chickens to eat. This method had some drawbacks:

- The chickens use a lot of their energy in walking around and keeping warm.
- There is a limit to the number of birds which can be kept in the farmyard.
- The farmyard becomes caked with chicken manure which is unpleasant and a breeding ground for germs and pests.

Free range chickens are usually kept in small numbers.

If you visit a modern poultry farm today you will see no chickens at first sight. In the poultry farm in Figure A there are thousands of chickens. Yet all that can be seen is a line of long, low buildings. This is a *broiler* farm. The chickens are kept inside these buildings all their lives. The building is kept at a constant temperature and is completely sterile so that no disease can enter. The chickens are fed on concentrated feed pellets and are injected with drugs to increase their growth rate so that they are ready to be sold when they are eight weeks old. There may be 20 000 chickens crowded into each building. About a hundred die each week, most of them from heart failure because they grow too quickly.

Egg-producing hens are kept in *battery farms*. There may be over 50 000 hens in each building. The temperature and humidity of the buildings are carefully controlled. The battery hens are contained within tiny cages. Several hens may be packed into each cage.

Figure A (*top*) A modern poultry farm – not a chicken in sight

Figure B (*bottom*) Inside the broiler house

Figure C Battery hens

They do not have room to turn round or even to stretch their wings. The cages are stacked in tiers. The hens are fed from a conveyor belt which passes the front of the cage. Their eggs and body waste are collected by another conveyor belt at the rear of the cage. Each battery hen produces an average of 224 eggs per year.

Nearly all of the eggs and chicken meat sold in Britain comes from factory farms, and an increasing proportion of our beef and pig products. These intensive methods mean that livestock production costs are greatly reduced (Figure E) and that more can be produced. This makes food cheaper in the shops. Factory farming has been criticized by some people who say that it is cruel to treat animals in this way.

British farming is highly intensive and highly scientific. Selective breeding and artificial insemination have improved the quality of livestock. Factory farming has increased livestock production. Artificial fertilisers, soil conditioners, insecticides and pesticides have raised crop yields. Higher yielding and disease-resistant strains of crops have been developed. Farm machinery has replaced human labour.

The efficient scientific methods of farming introduced in recent years have led to a rapid growth in food production. Less food is imported into Britain. Over half the food eaten in Britain is now home-produced (Figure D).

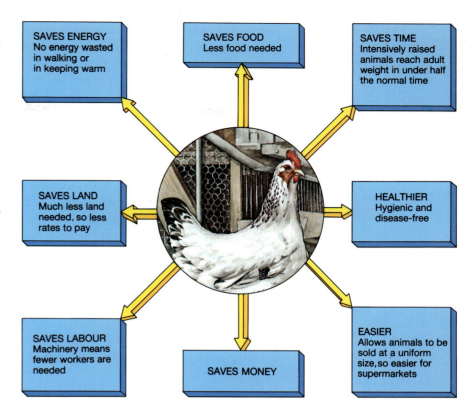

Figure E The advantages of intensive farming

Figure D Percentage of food eaten in Britain which is produced in Britain

Food	Percentage produced in Britain	
	1957	1986
Wheat	21	101
Barley	87	126
Meat	63	88
Bacon and ham	42	45
Eggs	99	100
Fresh milk	100	100
Butter	11	66
Cheese	48	70
Oils and fats	16	58
Sugar	19	54

QUESTIONS

1. a) Describe the free range method of poultry farming.
   b) What disadvantages does the free range method have?
   c) Can you think of any advantages which the free range method has?
   d) Some people are prepared to pay much more to buy free range eggs rather than eggs from battery farms. Why do you think this is?

2. Describe a modern battery chicken farm.

3. What are the advantages of factory farms?

4. Study Figure D.
   a) Draw a bar graph to show the ten foods in 1957 and 1986. Use two bars for each food, one for 1957 and one for 1986.
   b) Describe and try to explain the pattern revealed by the bar graph.

5. What are your views on factory farming of livestock? Using a sheet of A4 paper produce a pamphlet designed to *either* support *or* oppose factory farming. You should consider the arguments for and against factory farming in each case. Make your own views clear.

2.7 The Common Agricultural Policy

Figure A shows a British warehouse full of grain. Carefully grown and harvested by some of the most modern farming techniques in the world, this grain is stored because it cannot find a buyer. In a world where millions starve to death each year the warehouse is a silent witness to the over-production of European cereal farmers. It is a part of the 'grain mountain' of the European Community (EC). The 'grain mountain' is a result of the EC's Common Agricultural Policy (CAP). Grain is not the only crop which is over-produced by the EC's farmers. There is also a 'milk lake', a 'wine lake', a 'butter mountain' and a 'beef mountain'. The EC's over-production could create a whole new country of mountains, hills and lakes!

Why, and how, does the CAP create mountains and lakes of food? The EC Commission sets a *target price* for each product. Food imports into the EC are taxed to raise their price to the target price; in this way EC farmers cannot be undercut by cheap imports.

Products are sold on an open market within the EC, however, and the target price may not be reached for some products, especially if there is a surplus. Farmers are thus forced to accept prices lower than the target. For this reason the Commission sets a second price, the *intervention price*, below which prices are not allowed to fall. If the price of a product does fall below the intervention price then the EC guarantees to buy the product at the intervention price. The produce is then stored and, in theory, sold when market prices rise again. In practice, the produce is often sold at a loss. This is how the milk lake, butter mountain and beef mountain appear: produce purchased at intervention price which fills warehouses throughout the EC. If the produce is sold at a loss on world markets the EC is criticized by other countries, such as the USA, which accuse it of subsidising exports. If the produce is given away as aid to developing countries it may put local farmers out of business.

The price controls provide farmers with an assured market and income, and provide reliable food supplies for the consumer at a reasonable price. The CAP has been criticized:

- For encouraging over-production. Farmers know that they will receive a guaranteed price for their produce and so they campaign strongly for a high target price to be set.
- For encouraging inefficiency. The CAP protects small farmers who would otherwise be forced out of business.
- For damaging poorer countries. For example, developing countries whose economies are based on sugar cane have found it harder to export sugar to the EC countries because of the subsidising of sugar beet production by the CAP.
- For encouraging national interests before EC interests. Each government concentrates on the needs of its own farmers rather than of the EC as a whole.

Defenders of the CAP point out that the CAP is a social policy as well as an economic policy. Without the CAP the problems of unemployment and rural depopulation in the EC would be made much worse. The CAP has also made money available to modernize agriculture.

> **What is the CAP?**
> The countries of the EC agreed to the CAP in 1962. The CAP had three main aims:
> 1. To protect the income of farmers
> 2. To increase farm production and so reduce food imports
> 3. To ensure reasonable prices for consumers
>
> Seventy per cent of the EC's budget is spent on the CAP.

Figure A A hangar full of EC grain

The EC countries finally moved towards reform of the CAP in the mid-1980s. In 1984 quotas for milk production were introduced in an attempt to reduce the size of the milk lake. This marked the first real step towards controlling over-production. It caused hardship for many European milk producers and forced the slaughter of many dairy cows. Despite the strong opposition from many farmers the EC moved on to tackle the other sectors of gross over-production.

Some effects of the CAP on British agriculture

The EC subsidises *oilseed rape* production because it wants to reduce vegetable oil imports. Before Britain entered the EC, only 8000 hectares of rape were grown. By 1986 280 000 hectares were grown making it the third most important crop in Britain after barley and wheat. This bright yellow crop is now grown in almost every county in Britain. The black seeds are crushed to extract oil which is used for cooking oil, margarine and salad dressing. The residue contains proteins and is sold to animal feed manufacturers.

Field peas have become an important break crop (crop grown to break the rotation) since the CAP introduced a subsidy in 1980. By 1986 60 000 hectares were under field peas. The peas can be harvested by combine harvester and used for animal feed.

In recent years the *lupin* has become important as a farm crop through the influence of the CAP. The seeds can be an ingredient in animal feedstuffs. The residue is rich in nitrogen and can be ploughed back into the soil or fed directly to animals.

The 'sheepmeat regime' introduced in 1980 raised the guaranteed price for lamb by a quarter. This led to a rapid increase in the number of *sheep* in the UK from 29.8 million in 1979 to 35.1 million by 1984.

The introduction of milk quotas in 1984 led to a rapid decrease in the number of *dairy cattle* in Britain. Total cattle numbers fell from 13.3 million in 1983 to 11.9 million in 1986.

Figure B

Figure C One obvious effect of the CAP – English fields ablaze with oilseed rape

The Lomé Convention

An extension of the CAP has been the negotiations with certain developing countries under the Lomé Convention of 1975, which was extended for a period of five years in both 1980 and 1985. These countries, mostly ex-colonies of EC nations, receive guaranteed tariff-free entry for their basic exports such as sugar, bananas, rum and beef. Aid arrangements also exist. This assures the EC of a reliable supply of foodstuffs and raw materials which it cannot produce itself.

QUESTIONS

1. a) What do the initials CAP stand for?
   b) What are the three main aims of the CAP?
2. What are the following: a) target price b) intervention price?
3. What do you understand by the terms 'grain mountain' and 'milk lake'?
4. a) What is the connection between bright yellow fields and the EC?
   b) What other effects has the CAP had on British agriculture?
5. Write a letter to your local MEP (Member of the European Parliament) stating your views on the Common Agricultural Policy and the food surpluses within the EC.
6. How has the CAP been defended?
7. a) What is the Lomé Convention?
   b) What are the advantages of the Lomé Convention (i) for the developing countries who have signed the Convention (ii) for the EC nations?

Unit 2 ASSESSMENT

The following questions refer to Figure A:

1. Name one region of Britain where this hill farming area could be located. (1 mark)
2. What type of farming would you expect to be practised in the area? (1 mark)
3. State one change which has taken place in the number of farms. (1 mark)
4. What effect has this had on the amount of land being farmed? (1 mark)
5. What changes have taken place in the farm buildings? (4 marks)
6. a) What change do you think has taken place in the number of people employed in farming in this area? (1 mark)
   b) Why do you think this change has occurred? (3 marks)
7. Describe three other changes which have occurred and try to say why they happened. (9 marks)
8. Explain why conservationists might object to two of the changes that have taken place. (6 marks)

The following questions do not refer to Figure A:

9. Draw a cross-section of a Norwegian fjordside farm. Label your cross-section to include: the infield, the outfield, the saeter, the fjeld, the fjord, the farmhouse, area of coniferous trees. (10 marks)
10. What problems do (a) relief and (b) climate pose for Norwegian fjordside farmers? (6 marks)
11. Many farmers in East Anglia have removed hedgerows to create larger fields.
    a) Why have they done this? (4 marks)
    b) Why might the following organizations not welcome the removal of hedgerows:
       (i) The Royal Society for the Protection of Birds
       (ii) The Council for the Preservation of Rural England? (6 marks)

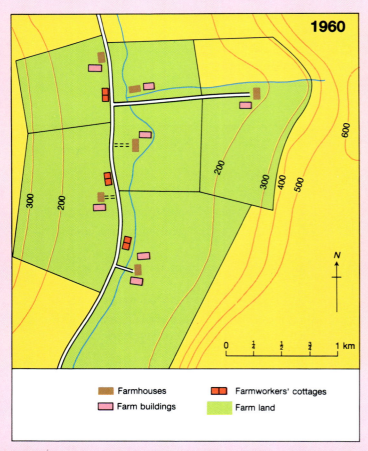
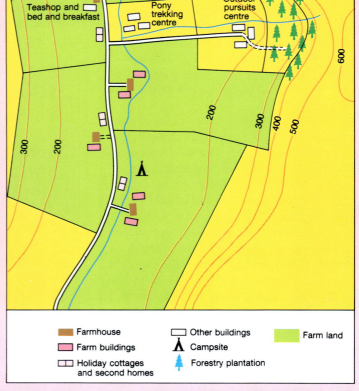

Figure A The same hill farming area in 1960 and 1990

12 'Modern farming practices endanger the environment in several ways. The use of chemical pesticides and insecticides has led to the build-up of harmful chemicals in the soil. The chemicals can be washed by the rain into rivers and subsequently into human water supplies. Over-ploughing and the removal of hedgerows has encouraged wind-blown soil erosion. EC farms are losing nearly one billion tonnes of topsoil per year. The destruction of copses and hedgerows has removed vital wildlife habitats and endangered many species.'
a) What are the threats posed by the use of chemicals in arable farming? (2 marks)
b) How has modern farming caused increased erosion of topsoil? (2 marks)
c) Why is the loss of wildlife habitats important? (4 marks)

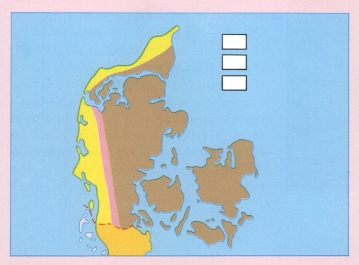

Figure B Glacial deposits in Denmark

13 a) Copy the map of Denmark (Figure B) and fill in the key. (3 marks)
b) Denmark was affected by an ice sheet during the Ice Age. Draw a large arrow on your map to show the direction from which the ice came. (1 mark)
c) Shade in the area of Denmark which was covered by ice. (1 mark)
d) How are glacial outwash deposits formed? (2 marks)
e) The soils on the outwash deposits are infertile. How have the Danish farmers improved the soils? (2 marks)
f) What is a farming co-operative association and what is its purpose? (5 marks)

TOTAL: 75 marks

Details for pupil profile sheet Unit 2

Knowledge and understanding

1. Hill farm
2. EC and government financial aid to farmers
3. Fjord, deltaic flat, strandflat
4. North Atlantic Drift
5. Transhumance
6. Agri-business
7. Contract farming
8. Co-operative associations in farming
9. Factory farming, broiler and battery hens
10. Food surpluses, grain mountain, milk lake

Skills

1. Complete a simple farm system diagram
2. Draw a pie graph
3. Draw a divided bar graph
4. Draw a line graph
5. Written description from a photograph
6. Drawing climatic graphs
7. Drawing a bar graph
8. Presenting textual information in the form of a table
9. Interpret change over time from graphs
10. Interpret change over time from maps

Values

1. Awareness of contrasting attitudes to intensive farming
2. Awareness of contrasting attitudes to food surpluses

3.1 Nomadic herders

Unit 3: Third World agriculture

Much of West Africa is covered with grassland called the savanna. This is the land of the Fulani people. Their ancestors moved eastwards from Senegal over six hundred years ago. They fought many battles to conquer large areas of West Africa. In northern Nigeria, for example, a series of 'jihads' (holy wars) defeated the powerful Hausa people. The Fulani became the ruling class and their religion, Islam, was adopted by the Hausa.

The Fulani were nomads. They roamed the savanna with their herds of cattle, sheep and goats in search of grazing and water. They carried all their possessions on the back of an ox and lived in temporary shelters like tents. They could not move too far south because of the tsetse fly which carries the killer cattle disease called sleeping sickness. They could not move too far north because of the semi-desert conditions on the margins of the Sahara. The lives of the Fulani were ruled by the climate of the savanna (Figure C). During the dry season they moved southwards into moister areas, during the wet season they moved northwards into the drier regions. Most Fulani used surplus milk and butter to buy corn in village markets. The Fulani looked on their cattle as status symbols – the more cattle a man owned, the more

Figure A Fulani stop at one of their regular water holes in Niger

Figure B West African savanna – the home of the Fulani

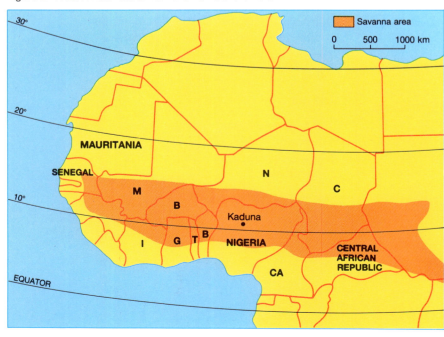

Figure C The climate of Kaduna, Nigeria

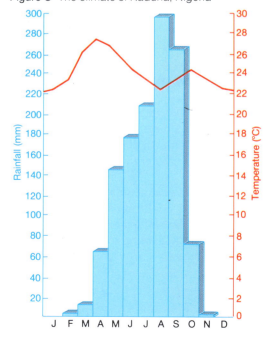

important the man was. Usually only old and weak cows were ever killed.

By the 1980s most Fulani are no longer nomads. They have settled in permanent homes for several reasons:

- Many lost their animals in droughts. The Sahel drought of the 1970s killed over 90 per cent of the cattle in Mauritania and destroyed the nomadic society. The 1983–87 drought added to the misery of the Fulani across much of West Africa.
- Pests and diseases have attacked the cattle herds. Rinderpest has killed many cattle in recent years.
- As more of the land is used for growing crops, farmers fence off their fields to keep the Fulani's cattle away.
- The building of dams and reservoirs for hydro-electric power and irrigation schemes has cut the traditional routes of the Fulani in several countries.

The Fulani who have settled grow a range of crops for subsistence and for sale. These include millet, yams, maize, beans and ground nuts. They still keep cattle, but are increasingly treating them as a source of money rather than of status. There is a growing demand for beef and dairy products from the cities of West Africa. Most West African governments are encouraging the nomads to settle down, improve their pastures and produce beef, dairy products and cash crops. There is a growing traffic in cattle by train and lorry from the savanna areas to the coastal cities where the animals are slaughtered. The Fulani may now earn good money from their farming and can buy a wider range of goods including clothes, kitchen utensils, radios and so on. Some fortunate Fulani have now taken to driving around in Land Rovers and Land Cruisers rather than walking or riding on horseback.

The traditional nomadic way of life is rapidly dying out. Most Fulani now live settled lives as farmers. Others have left the countryside altogether and gone to seek work in the growing towns.

Figure D Most Fulani have now settled in permanent villages like this one near Bida in Niger

QUESTIONS

1. a) Where do the Fulani live?
   b) What is their religion?
2. 'The Fulani were nomads.' What does this mean?
3. Copy the map (Figure B) and using an atlas to help you, name the countries shown by their first letters.
4. Why were the Fulani confined to the savanna zone?
5. Study Figure C and copy and complete the table below:

The savanna climate of Kaduna, Nigeria

| Lowest temperature (°C): |
| Highest temperature (°C): |
| Range of temperature (°C): |
| Total rainfall (mm): |
| Rainfall November–March (mm): |
| Rainfall April–October (mm): |

6. How does the Savanna climate affect the lives of the Fulani?
7. Explain why many Fulani have now settled in permanent homes.
8. How does the settled way of life differ from the traditional nomadic lifestyle of the Fulani?
9. Why do you think that African governments are encouraging the nomads to settle down?

3.2 Subsistence farming

Subsistence farmers grow food mainly to feed themselves and their families. Most farmers in India are subsistence farmers. Seventy-one per cent of the Indian working population is employed in agriculture.

The main crops of the Indian subsistence farmers are rice, wheat and millet. Rice is the main food of most of the people. One of the most productive areas is the basin of the River Ganges in India and Bangladesh. This is one of the densest areas of rural population in the world, supported by this highly successful form of subsistence farming. The soil is kept in good condition through the use of manure but without the need for expensive chemical fertilisers.

The paddy field is the main feature of this form of farming. The rice must be planted in a field with several centimetres of standing water. The land is divided by low earth banks into small fields. In the lower Ganges Basin the heavy monsoon rains are enough to flood the paddy fields. In the drier areas of the upper Ganges water is diverted into the fields from rivers.

In June the rice seeds are sown in nursery beds. The paddy fields are ploughed with the aid of water buffalo or bullocks pulling a simple wooden plough. In July the seedlings are transplanted by hand into the paddy fields. This is backbreaking work. The rice grows for four months during which time it is weeded and the water level is

Figure A Stages in the production of rice: bundles of rice seedlings ready for planting (*top left*), transplanting the rice seedlings into the flooded paddy fields (*top right*), harvesting (*bottom left*), threshing and winnowing (*bottom right*)

gradually reduced. The rice is harvested using hand sickles. The rice is taken to the villages for threshing. It is beaten by hand and trampled by animals to separate the grain from the straw. The grain is then winnowed by throwing it into the air to separate the grain from the chaff (husks).

Rice is grown during the wet season. A second crop may be grown during the dry season if irrigation water is available, or a cereal which can grow in the drier conditions such as wheat, barley or millet may be grown.

This form of subsistence farming has fed the people of the Ganges Basin for centuries, but the rapidly growing population has put the system under strain. The traditional farming methods cannot produce enough food to give everybody enough to eat. The diet of the average person in rural India is low in both calories and protein. This causes malnutrition which reduces a person's energy and reduces the amount of effort they can put into farming. A vicious circle of malnutrition is created (Figure C). If the monsoon fails the rice crop is reduced and the people go hungry. Severe droughts force people to leave their homes and move to the towns and cities in search of food.

New strains of rice which give higher yields have been developed. This is called the Green Revolution (see page 40). Unfortunately the new rice needs a lot of fertiliser and pesticide, so only the richer farmers can afford to grow it and they have been largely responsible for the rapid increase in Indian rice production from 60 million tonnes in 1973 to 108 million tonnes in 1990. Poverty, hard work and malnutrition remain the lot of most Indian subsistence farmers and their families.

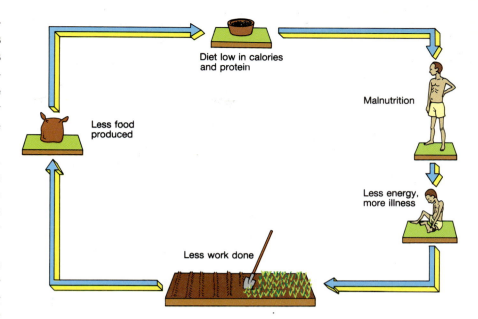

Figure C The vicious circle of malnutrition

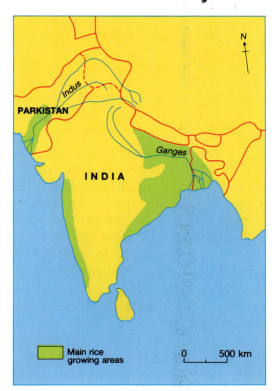

Figure B The main rice growing areas of India and Pakistan

QUESTIONS

1. What percentage of the Indian working population is employed in agriculture?
2. Where is the River Ganges?
3. Why can the basin of the River Ganges support a dense rural population?
4. List the main stages of rice production.
5. What other crops may be grown by the rice farmers?
6. What is meant by 'the vicious circle of malnutrition'?
7. Why is the traditional rice farming system of the Ganges Basin under strain?

3.3 Cash crops: plantations

Many developing countries depend upon the export of a few crops. Many of these cash crops were first exported by Europeans when the developing countries were colonies. The Europeans often forced the people to stop growing subsistence food crops and to grow crops which the Europeans themselves wanted. For example, in Tanzania millet was replaced by sisal, in the Gambia rice was replaced by peanuts and in Ghana sweet potatoes were replaced by cocoa. In order to force the people to grow cash crops the colonial governments imposed taxes on huts and land.

Cash crops are often grown on plantations which are large farms growing a single crop for sale. The first plantations were developed in Brazil and the West Indies for sugar cane. Later rubber, coffee, tea, cocoa, palm oil and sisal plantations were developed.

Plantations in Malaysia

Malaysia is the world's leading producer of rubber. Almost half of the rubber is grown on plantations. The rubber tree was introduced to Malaysia by the British. They had stolen rubber seeds from Brazil and smuggled them to Britain where they were raised in the hothouses of Kew Gardens. From there the seedlings were taken to Malaysia and Sri Lanka.

Figure A A Malaysian rubber plantation

Figure B Collecting rubber is a skilled task

The rubber is produced from latex, the sap in the bark of the rubber tree. The tree grows to a height of about 20 metres and yields up to 2 kilograms of rubber per year. When the tree is about five years old it is tapped. This is a skilled process. A thin section of bark is cut and the latex drips into a collecting cup.

The latex is collected every day. It is taken to the plantation factory where it is sieved, acetic acid is added to form a soft, spongy material which is then passed through rollers and cut into sheets. The sheets are dried in a smoke room or by hot-air driers. The dried rubber is then transported by train or lorry to the ports for export.

The plantations were designed to supply rubber cheaply to British factories. The workers were paid little and the system was tightly controlled for the benefit of Britain. Most of the money from the sale of rubber went to British companies rather than Malaysia. When Malaysia became independent some of the plantations were broken up and the land given to local farmers. Other plantations were taken over by the new government. Some others remained in the control of multi-national companies based in the developed countries.

Malaysia produces 40 per cent of the world's rubber. It is vulnerable to price cuts on the world market. Rubber has been replaced by synthetic rubber, a substance made from oil. The synthetic rubber is made by petrochemical plants in the developed countries. Less natural rubber is now needed by the developed countries. This is bad news for Malaysia because rubber makes up over one third of the country's exports.

Malaysia's response has been to develop plantations of oil-palm. The oil-palm is related to the coconut palm. Palm oil is used in margarine, cooking oil, soap, ice cream and animal feed. Palm oil production has increased dramatically in recent years. (Figure C) and Malaysia now produces over half of the world's palm oil. The plantations are run by the Malaysian government and by private companies. The Anglo-Dutch multi-national Unilever owns two of the largest plantations in Johore and Sabah covering nearly 14000 hectares. The company has built a processing factory, houses for the plantation employees, shops, a clinic and other services at the plantation villages. The plantations are run as a joint venture between Unilever and Malaysian interests.

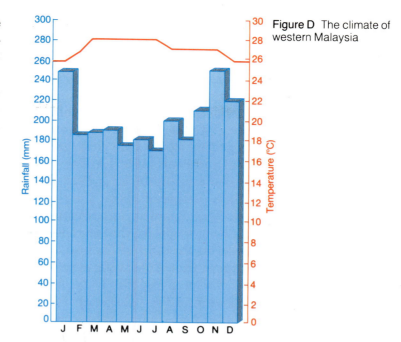

Figure D The climate of western Malaysia

Figure C Palm oil production in Malaysia

Year	Palm oil production (thousand tonnes)
1950	50
1955	80
1960	120
1965	155
1970	457
1975	1265
1980	2530
1985	3750
1990	6100

QUESTIONS

1 What is a plantation?

2 Study the table below:

The world's leading producers of rubber

Country	Production (thousand tonnes)
Malaysia	1 550
Indonesia	990
Thailand	540
India	170
China	135
Sri Lanka	135
Liberia	70
Philippines	70
Vietnam	50
Nigeria	45

a) On an outline map of the world shade in the areas of the ten countries in the table.
b) How would you describe the location of these ten countries?
c) Figure D shows the climate of western Malaysia, an area highly suited to rubber cultivation. Using the graph to help you, describe the climatic requirements of the rubber tree.

3 Describe the process of rubber production.

4 Why did the British develop rubber plantations in Malaysia?

5 a) Why has demand for rubber fallen?
b) What effect has this had on the price of rubber?

6 a) Draw a line graph to show the production of palm oil in Malaysia (see Figure C).
b) Explain why the recent rapid expansion of palm oil production in Malaysia has occurred.

3.4 Cash crops: cocoa

Where would we be without chocolate? The advertisements on TV and in the street encourage us to spend our money. How many chocolate bars have you eaten this week?

The main raw material for chocolate is cocoa. Cocoa cannot be grown in Britain. The cocoa tree first grew in Central and South America. The Aztecs of Mexico and the Incas of Peru drank chocolate prepared from their cocoa farms. The Spanish and Portuguese took cocoa seeds to the islands they occupied in the Gulf of Guinea. It was from there that African farmers introduced the crop to the West African mainland in 1879. Ghanaian farmers were the first major producers and Ghana became the world's chief supplier of cocoa by 1910. Since 1978 the Ivory Coast has overtaken Ghana.

Cocoa farming in the Ivory Coast

Large scale farming of cocoa in the Ivory Coast did not begin until the 1920s. Among the giants of the equatorial rain forest the cocoa tree is small, less than 8 metres high. It is similar in size and shape to an English apple tree. Figure C shows the conditions which the cocoa tree needs. Cocoa beans grow in bright orange pods about 20 cm long on the trunk and branches of the tree. The pods are shaped like a melon and they begin to appear when the tree is four years old.

There are two harvest periods, the main one between October and January which is the dry season and a secondary harvest between May and July in the rainy season. The pods are cut from the trees and are split open to reveal the white cocoa beans embedded in a sticky pulp. The following process then takes place:

1 The beans are scooped out of the pods and wrapped in banana leaves to ferment.

2 During fermentation the beans are thoroughly stirred each day.

3 After fermentation the beans are dried in the sun. This turns the white beans into a rich brown colour.

4 The beans are then packed into sacks and taken to the government-operated buying station where the beans are weighed, graded and purchased.

5 The cocoa is then transported by road or rail to the seaport of Abidjan for export to the UK, France, the USA and the Netherlands.

Most of the cocoa is grown by peasant farmers on small holdings of between 1 and 4 hectares. 400 000 farmers grow cocoa and most also grow coffee. The farms grow a range of food crops including bananas, pineapples, mangoes, avocados and aubergines. Over two million people are involved in the production of

Figure A

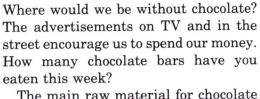

Requirements of the cocoa tree
- Rainfall varying from 1000 mm to 2500 mm; but the amount is less important than an even distribution.
- High temperatures, from 21°C to 32°C. Temperatures below 15°C will halt growth.
- Moist, light, well-drained soils.
- Shelter from strong winds.
- Shade in the early years of growth.

Figure C

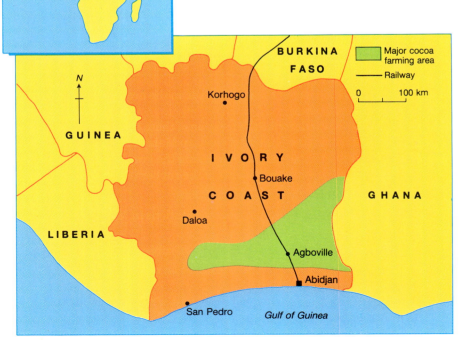

Figure B The cocoa farming area of the Ivory Coast

Figure D Raking the cocoa beans during fermentation

cocoa, from the families of farmers to the workers from neighbouring African countries who are hired to help with the land clearing or harvest.

Cocoa is vital to the Ivory Coast. It provides employment for over two million people and provides a third of the country's export earnings. Yet the Ivory Coast is at the mercy of the fluctuating world price of cocoa which is set by the developed countries who are the main customers for the cocoa. While the price of manufactured goods from the developed countries rises all the time, the price of cocoa rises and falls. This makes it very difficult for the Ivory Coast to plan for the future.

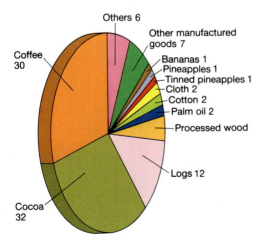

Figure E The export trade of the Ivory Coast (commodities and percentage of total export earnings)

QUESTIONS

1 Study the table below:

Major producers of cocoa

Country	Cocoa production (thousand tonnes)	Percentage of world total
Ivory Coast	411	24.7
Brazil	346	?
Ghana	188	?
Nigeria	160	?
Cameroon	115	?
Malaysia	93	?
Ecuador	60	?
Dominican Republic	44	?
Colombia	41	?
World Total	1660	100

a) Copy the table and complete the column showing percentage of world total.

b) On an outline map of the world draw in the nine countries in the table. Colour in each country and give your map the heading 'The world's major producers of cocoa'.

c) Describe the distribution of the major cocoa producing nations.

d) Try to explain why this distribution occurs.

2 Figure E shows the trade of the Ivory Coast in a recent year:

a) Construct a divided bar 100 mm long to illustrate the statistics in the pie chart. Give the bar a suitable title.

b) What percentage of the Ivory Coast's export earnings consists of manufactured goods? (In the pie chart these are commodities listed as processed wood, cloth, tinned pineapples and other manufactured goods.)

c) Why has the government of the Ivory Coast tried to encourage the growth of agricultural processing industries?

3 What effects would a varying price of cocoa have upon the Ivory Coast?

3.5 The big projects

Several developing countries have invested in large scale agricultural developments. These big projects have been intended to improve the countries' food production and transform their economies. Some of the largest schemes have taken place in the Sudan.

The Republic of Sudan is the largest country in Africa. It is over ten times the size of the UK, yet has a population of just over a third of the UK population. The northern half of the Sudan is desert.

The Sudan does have one priceless advantage: the River Nile. With water for irrigation even a desert can bloom. Simple lifting devices such as the sakia and shaduf (Figure B) have been used for centuries to raise water over the river's banks and transfer it to the fields. Each summer the Nile floods. The precious water is trapped by earth walls built around the fields. The flood waters slowly drain away depositing fertile silt in the fields.

In 1925 a dam was built across the Blue Nile at Sennar. The dam was built by the British as part of a big project to supply cotton cheaply to Britain's textile mills. The water can be released slowly over the year. This is called perennial irrigation. A canal carries the water into the Gezira area which lies between the rivers Blue Nile and White Nile south of Khartoum, the Sudan's capital. The water is distributed by a vast network of smaller canals and ditches around the Gezira. The scheme has transformed the Gezira from semi-desert into the largest single farming enterprise in Africa.

The soils of the Gezira were partly responsible for the success of the scheme. They are fine black silt carried by the Nile from volcanic areas in Ethiopia. The silt is impermeable and retains water in its upper layers when irrigated. The original Gezira scheme irrigated 120 000 hectares. This was

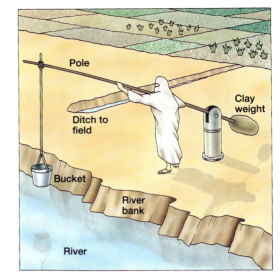

Figure B The shaduf – a traditional form of irrigation

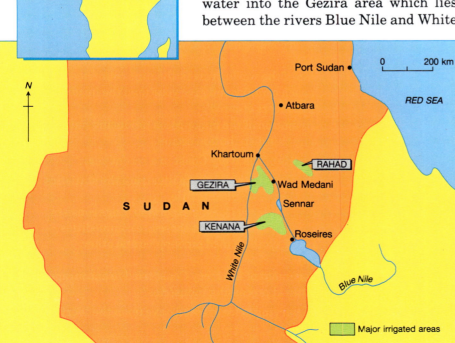

Figure A The main irrigated areas of the Sudan

Figure C A Gezira farmer works on the muddy banks of an irrigation canal in a sorghum field

Figure D The Gezira area from space. The ERTS false-colour satellite image shows the fields in shades of red. (This photograph is made up of two separate satellite images spliced together – one is slightly darker than the other.)

increased to 900 000 hectares when the Managil extension was completed during the 1960s. A new dam was built at Roseires 200 km south of Sennar to provide water for the extensions. Both the dams at Sennar and Roseires produce hydro-electric power. Roseires alone produces 60 per cent of the Sudan's total HEP.

Cotton is the Gezira's major crop. Seventy per cent of the Sudan's cotton is grown there and provides the Sudan with its major source of money from exports. The Gezira is also the Sudan's major food producing area. It produces 50 per cent of the country's wheat, 30 per cent of the lubia beans, 25 per cent of the peanuts and 15 per cent of the sorghum. A vast sugar cane estate and a beef cattle ranch have also been developed.

The potential for agricultural production in the Sudan is great. It is estimated that 50 million hectares could be cultivated compared with the current six million. Yet in the 1980s many of the Sudanese people were threatened by starvation. A long and bloody civil war in the south of the country disrupted the economy. The long drought cut food production outside the irrigated areas. The cash crops grown in the irrigated area are a vital source of income for the Sudan, but much of the money is being spent on fighting the civil war rather than on developing the country. The Sudan's irrigated areas could feed much of Africa, but a vast amount of money would be needed to support the change from cash crops to food crops. And the war drags on.

QUESTIONS

1 a) Where is the Republic of Sudan?

2 a) Find a population map of Africa in your atlas. Describe the distribution of population in the Sudan.
b) Try to explain the distribution of population.

3 a) Make a copy of Figure B.
b) How does the shaduf work?
c) What advantages and disadvantages does the shaduf have as a means of irrigation?

4 Study the table below:

Climate statistics of Khartoum, Sudan

Month:	J	F	M	A	M	J	J	A	S	O	N	D
Temperature (°C)	22	25	30	32	34	35	33	30	31	30	30	26
Rainfall (mm):	0	0	1	2	4	12	55	73	22	5	2	0

a) Draw a line graph to show the temperature statistics and a bar graph to show the rainfall statistics.
b) What is the lowest temperature and in which month does it occur?
c) What is the highest temperature and in which month does it occur?
d) What is the total annual rainfall?
e) What problems would this climate cause for a farmer?
f) Find a climate graph for London, England in your atlas. How does London's climate compare with that of Khartoum?

3.6 An uncertain future

'Food for All!'; 'New Super Seeds Promise End to World Hunger'; 'Miracle Rice!' These were claims made in the 1960s for a process which has been called the Green Revolution.

The most dramatic advances have been made in rice production. Ninety per cent of the world's rice is grown in South-East Asia. Until the 1960s increases in rice production were only achieved through opening up new areas for farming. In 1965 the International Rice Research Institute (IRRI) based in the Philippines introduced a new variety of rice seed called IR8. This was a hybrid seed created by cross-breeding existing seeds. IR8 gave higher yields than other rices. Many other new varieties of rice have been introduced since 1965. One of the most recent, IR64, yields over 10 tonnes per hectare compared with an average 2 tonnes per hectare for older varieties. The new seeds have been largely responsible for a remarkable increase in world rice production since 1965 (see Figure B).

Figure A The higher yield of the new varieties of rice is clear in this photograph

Figure B World rice production since 1960

Year	Rice production (million tonnes)	Percentage increases over previous five years
1960	242	
1965	254	5
1970	311	22
1975	343	10
1980	396	15
1985	466	18

Notice that between 1960 and 1965 world rice production increased by only 5 per cent, but following the introduction of the new rice seeds production increased by 22 per cent over the five year period up to 1970. The increases in

Figure C Rice production in selected countries

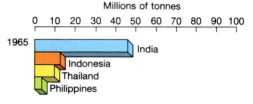
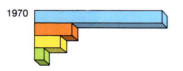
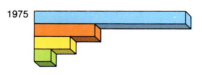

Figure D World rice production in 1990

Country	Rice production (million tonnes)
China	179
India	108
Indonesia	44
Bangladesh	27
Thailand	22
Vietnam	18
Burma	14
Japan	13
Brazil	11
Philippines	10
World Total	506

some countries were dramatic (Figure C). Countries which imported rice in the 1960s, such as India and Indonesia, were actually able to export rice by the 1980s. Wages for many rice labourers were increased as profits rose.

Success – or failure?

Clearly the Green Revolution has led to a rapid increase in rice production. However, it has not been a complete success. This is because of the special and expensive requirements of the new rice:

- High quality, well irrigated land. Too much or too little water will kill the rice.
- The new rice needs large amounts of chemical fertiliser to produce the best yields.
- The new rice is vulnerable to pests and diseases. Large amounts of pesticide and herbicide are needed.
- The use of mechanical weeders, combine harvesters and diesel pumps produces highest yields.

Only the richer farmers could afford to use the new rice, the poor peasants with only small farms could not. Some peasants who tried by borrowing money fell into debt and went bankrupt.

The large estates of the wealthy farmers in South-East Asia have forced many peasant smallholders out of business. Increasing use of machines has reduced the number of farming jobs. Much of the rice is sold to the wealthier people in the cities, fed to animals or exported to developed countries. This is not the best way to develop agriculture in the developing world. It means that the few rich are getting richer while the many poor are getting poorer.

So what can be done to spread the benefits of the Green Revolution to the poor? Land reform is needed to break up the big estates and give the land to the poor so that they own their own land and have larger farms. Peasant co-operatives would allow the cheaper bulk purchase of seed, fertiliser and pesticide and the shared purchase of machinery. The traditional farming methods should be improved rather than replaced by less suitable mechanised farming. Stronger, disease-resistant seeds needing less water should be developed.

Figure E Terraced rice fields, part of a large estate in Bali, Indonesia

QUESTIONS

1 What do you understand by the term 'Green Revolution'?

2 What are hybrid seeds?

3 List three ways in which the Green Revolution has been successful.

4 a) Copy Figure C and add the production for 1980 and 1985:

Country	1980	1985	Country	1980	1985
India	80	92	Thailand	17	20
Indonesia	30	39	Philippines	8	8

b) Try to explain the shape of the graph.

5 a) Study Figure D and draw a bar graph to illustrate the statistics.
b) What percentage of total world rice production is grown in the ten leading countries?
c) Shade in the ten countries listed in the table on an outline map of the world.
d) Describe the location of the major rice producing nations. Why is rice production concentrated in such a limited area of the world?

6 'The Green Revolution has succeeded only in making the rich richer and the poor poorer.' What does this statement mean? What evidence is there to support the statement?

Unit 3 ASSESSMENT

1 'The Fulani were nomads. They roamed the savanna with their herds of cattle, sheep and goats in search of grazing and water. The lives of the Fulani were ruled by the climate of the savanna.'
   a) Who are the Fulani? (1 mark)
   b) In which continent do the Fulani live? (1 mark)
   c) What is a 'nomad'? (2 marks)
   d) What do you understand by the word 'savanna'? (2 marks)
   e) Describe the main features of the savanna climate and say how they affected the lives of the Fulani nomads. (6 marks)

2 a) What is a paddy field? (1 mark)
   b) What are the main stages of rice production? (6 marks)

3 Using examples from developing countries, describe and explain the differences between subsistence and commercial types of farming. (7 marks)

Figure A The major coffee producing countries

Figure B (*inset*) The production of these countries

4 Study the table below:

The monsoon climate of the Ganges Delta

Month	J	F	M	A	M	J	J	A	S	O	N	D
Temperature (°C)	21	22	25	33	32	30	28	30	29	28	25	21
Rainfall (mm)	5	15	20	45	125	285	330	340	250	120	25	10

   a) Name the hottest month. (1 mark)
   b) What is the annual range of temperature? (1 mark)
   c) What is the wettest month? (1 mark)
   d) What is the total annual rainfall? (2 marks)
   e) Draw a line graph to show the monthly temperatures. (6 marks)
   f) (i) What is unusual about the pattern of monthly temperature between April and September? (1 mark)
      (ii) What might explain this unusual pattern? (2 marks)
   g) What problems might the monsoon climate pose for farmers in the Ganges Delta? (4 marks)

5 a) What is the 'Green Revolution'? (3 marks)
   b) What have been the successes and failures of the Green Revolution? (8 marks)

MAJOR PRODUCERS OF COFFEE (1984)

Country	Annual Production (thousand tonnes)
Brazil	1 353
Colombia	780
Indonesia	330
Mexico	270
Ethiopia	240
Uganda	210
El Salvador	170
Philippines	150
Guatemala	140
Cameroon	130

In the following questions five possible answers are given. Choose the best answer in each case:

6 Rinderpest is
  A A nomadic people living in West Africa.
  B A breed of cattle especially suited to the savanna.
  C A religious holy war.
  D A large dam built on the River Blue Nile.
  E A disease affecting cattle in Africa. (1 mark)

7 Rice is winnowed by
  A Beating the plant to separate the grain from the straw.
  B Using improved strains of the crop.
  C Applying fertiliser to the soil.
  D Throwing it into the air to separate the grain from the chaff.
  E Water buffalo or bullocks pulling a wooden plough. (1 mark)

8 The sap in the bark of the rubber tree is called
  A Sisal.   D Acetic acid.
  B Latex.   E Palm oil.
  C Unilever. (1 mark)

9 Which of the following statements does not apply to the Sudan Gezira Project?
  A The Gezira lies between the White Nile and the Blue Nile.
  B The major crop grown is cotton.
  C The Gezira receives water from dams at Sennar, Aswan and Roseires.
  D The soils of the area are fine black silt which retain water when irrigated.
  E Other important crops grown in the Gezira include wheat, peanuts and sorghum. (1 mark)

10 Which of the following countries is not a major producer of rice?
  A Indonesia.   D India.
  B Papua New Guinea. E Bangladesh.
  C China. (1 mark)

11 The map (Figure A) shows the top ten producers of coffee. Figure B is a table which shows the production of these ten countries.
  a) Link the ten letters on the map with the correct country from the table. (5 marks)
  b) Draw a bar graph to illustrate the statistics in the table. (5 marks)
  c) Much coffee is grown in plantations. Describe the system of plantation farming. (5 marks)

TOTAL: 75 marks

Details for pupil profile sheet Unit 3

Knowledge and understanding

1 Savanna
2 Nomadic farming
3 Paddy field, transplanting, threshing, winnowing rice
4 Monsoon climate
5 Malnutrition
6 Green Revolution
7 Hybrid seeds
8 Irrigation

Skills

1 Interpreting a climatic graph
2 Draw a line graph
3 Interpret a map of population density from an atlas
4 Mark countries on an outline map, using atlas
5 Written description from a photograph
6 Drawing climatic graphs
7 Drawing a bar graph
8 Interpret change over time from tables

Values

1 Awareness of change affecting pastoral nomads
2 Awareness of role of European colonial powers in change from subsistence to cash crops in developing countries and the effect on food supply
3 Awareness of trade imbalances between developed and developing countries

4.1 Introduction

Unit 4: The industrial system

What is industry? Which of the people in these photographs is working in industry?

The answer is ... all of them are working in industry. The word 'industry' is often taken to mean only making things, but this is more correctly called *manufacturing* and is only a part of industry. Industry means any form of employment which involves using or

Figure A

The three sectors of industry
Primary industry means those industries which produce raw materials and includes farming, fishing, forestry and mining.
Secondary industry means those industries which make things from raw materials. They are often called manufacturing industries.
Tertiary industry means those industries which provide a service to other industry and to people. It includes transport, retailing, administration and public services. Tertiary industries are often called service industries.

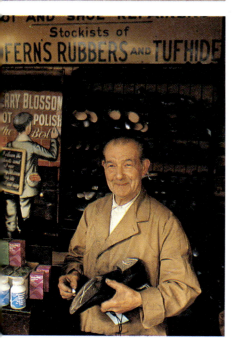

producing goods and services. It includes manufacturing, trade, commerce, agriculture, education, entertainment and many other activities.

It is clear that industry is a very broad term covering a wide range of activities. It is usual to divide industry into three sectors as shown in Figure A. The sectors are closely related. Consider this book, for example:

- The raw materials for the book come from the forests of Norway. The growing and felling of the trees is a primary industry.
- The wood is processed into pulp in Norway then shipped to the UK where it is turned into paper in a paper mill. This is a secondary industry. China clay, quarried in Cornwall, is added to the paper.
- Tertiary industries then took over. A person in an office in Oxford then ordered the paper to print the book on. The author typed the manuscript into his word processor at his home and the book editor and others in their Oxford offices supervised the final version. Photographs were taken or obtained. Artists made sense of the author's maps and diagrams. Secondary industry then becomes involved again as the book is printed. The manuscript and artwork were flown out to Hong Kong where the book was printed and then shipped back to England. Lorries distributed the book to shops and warehouses and then on to the customers. At each stage, people in offices filled in forms and signed papers concerning the book.

The publication of this book involved hundreds of people in dozens of different jobs in primary, secondary and tertiary industry. This is typical of most of the goods which we buy.

QUESTIONS

1. What does the word 'industry' mean?
2. Study the list of industries and jobs below and list them as primary, secondary or tertiary industry:
   electronics, aluminium smelting, frozen vegetables, forestry, plumber, shop assistant, car assembly, hairdresser, footballer, policeman, insurance, iron and steel, limestone quarrying, banking, soldier, musician, shepherd, leather goods, fishing, acting, nurse.
3. Study the table below:

Employment in Britain

Type of industry	Total employees (thousands)	Percentage of total
Agriculture	308	1.5
Forestry	19	0.1
Fishing	18	0.1
Mining and quarrying	324	1.6
Total Primary	**669**	**3.3**
Food, drink & tobacco	591	2.9
Chemicals	410	2.0
Metal manufacture	298	1.5
Engineering	2005	10.0
Cars	307	1.5
Aerospace	190	0.9
Textiles & clothing	644	3.2
Construction	999	5.0
Other manufacturing	1122	5.6
Total Secondary	**5600**	**32.9**
Gas, electricity & water	320	1.6
Transport and communications	1357	6.8
Distribution	2514	12.5
Financial and professional services	7105	35.4
Public administration and the armed services	1504	7.5
Total Tertiary	**13800**	**63.8**

a) Draw a bar graph with three bars showing the percentage of total employment in primary, secondary and tertiary industry.
b) Which type of primary industry employs the most people?
c) Which three types of secondary industry employ the most people?
d) Which two types of tertiary industry employ the most people?

4. Draw a flow diagram to show the different industries involved in the publication of this book. Use a different colour for primary, secondary and tertiary industries.

4.2 Industry as a system

Industry operates to create wealth or to provide a public service. Some industries manage to do both. The creation of wealth is very important since it pumps money into the country's economy and encourages the economy to grow (Figure A).

All industry works as a system with inputs, processes and outputs. On page 36 we studied the cocoa industry. One of the main products of the cocoa industry is chocolate. Figure C shows the system which operates in the production of chocolate at Cadbury, Britain's largest chocolate manufacturer. Its inputs are cocoa, milk, sugar and flavourings and its outputs are a range of chocolate products, plus profits, wages and taxes.

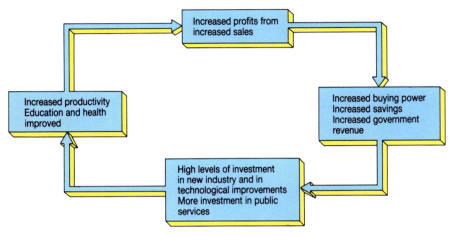

Figure A The cycle of wealth creation

Figure B The end of the manufacturing process – chocolate bars roll off the production line

Industry works as a system at a variety of scales. At the smallest level are workshop and cottage industries which employ only a handful of people. These are usually craft industries, and usually involve working at home. An example is pottery produced in rural areas of Britain and aimed at the tourist market. Often machines will be used in such cottage industries and the skills involved may have been relearnt from an earlier time. In the developing world cottage industries are very important. Weaving is a major example. The village workshop will feature hand looms, simple machines using traditional skills. Such weaving will be aimed mainly at a subsistence level to support the weaver and his or her family.

Most manufacturing industry operates a factory system. Large factories first became common during the period called the Industrial Revolution in Britain. After about AD 1750 the introduction of large steam-powered machines burning coal meant that large buildings called factories had to be built to house them. Factories remain the most important type of manufacturing building today, but their design has changed considerably since the days of the early steam-powered mills with their tall chimneys and forbidding appearance. Most factories are now much pleasanter buildings to look at and work in. Increased automation has meant that fewer people are needed in factories; in some modern factories almost all the work is done by machine.

Cadbury operates three large factories in the production of chocolate. Cadbury is just part of a much larger, *multi-national company* called Cadbury Schweppes which also manufactures soft drinks. Cadbury Schweppes employs 13 000 people in the UK and 15 000 more throughout the world, and has major factories in the USA, India, Nigeria, Australia, New Zealand and South Africa.

Cadbury Schweppes is a large and important company, but by the standards of multi-national corporations

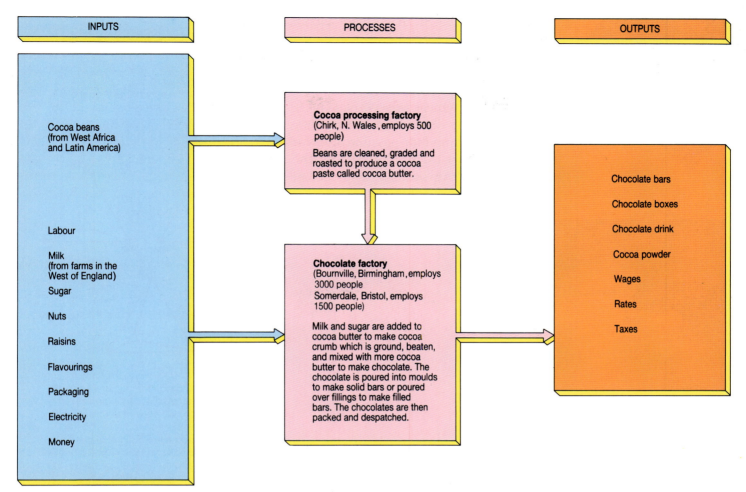

Figure C The industrial system – making chocolate

it is quite small. The largest multi-national company with its headquarters in Britain is the Shell oil company which employs 160 000 people throughout the world. Multi-national companies have great power and wealth. In 1985 Shell had a turnover of £70 000 million – that is more than the Gross Domestic Product for such countries as Argentina, Belgium, Egypt, Nigeria and Pakistan! There are several US multi-nationals larger than Shell.

From the weaver's cottage to the multi-national corporation's worldwide factories is a great progression, but they are both part of an industrial system which embraces us all.

QUESTIONS

1. What is the purpose of 'industry'?
2. What is meant by the term 'cottage industry'?
3. Copy the diagram below of an industrial system and add the following labels in the correct places:
   wages, raw materials, electricity, products, packaging, rates, labour, processes, taxes

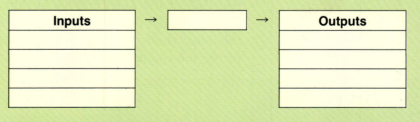

4. What is a 'multi-national' company?
5. How does industry create wealth?
6. Using examples, explain how cottage industries differ between developed and developing countries.
7. Explain the operation of the industrial system developed in the manufacture of chocolate.
8. What advantages and disadvantages do you think Cadbury get from being a part of a multi-national company?

4.3 Industrial location 1

Figure A shows St. Augustine Island where Prangley Bread Ltd is going to build a new bakery. The bakery uses flour which is imported to the island through the two ports of Surf Bay and Littleport. The most important market for bread is the city of Barton. Prangley Bread is studying four possible sites for its new bakery, A, B, C and D on the map. Answer questions 1–3 before reading on.

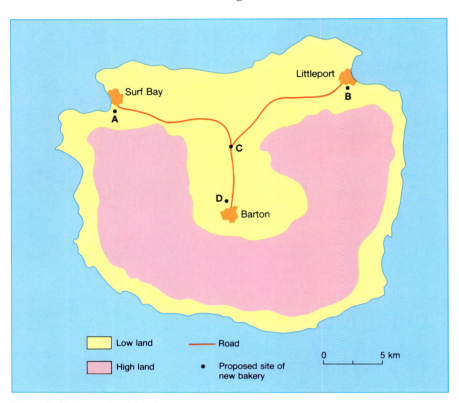

Figure A St. Augustine Island

A number of theories have been developed to explain the location of industry. One of the most famous is that of Weber (Figure B). This was based on the idea that industry will be sited where the company's costs are lowest.

QUESTIONS

1. Working with your neighbour list the advantages and disadvantages of each of the four sites A, B, C and D for the location of a bakery.
2. Decide which of the four sites you would recommend for the location of the bakery and give your reasons.
3. What other information would it be useful to know about the island and the four possible locations before making a final decision on the site for the bakery?

Weber's theory of industrial location

Weber assumed that:
- industry will locate where costs are lowest (the 'least-cost' location)
- transport costs vary with the weight of a product and the distance it is transported
- there is no political interference

Weber used triangles to find the least-cost location:

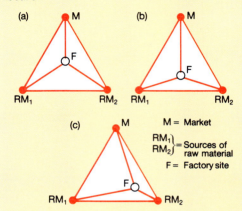

In (a) transport costs are equal for raw materials and the finished product – so the factory is located at the centre of the triangle.
In (b) the weight of the raw materials is higher than that of the finished product – so the factory is located nearer the raw materials.
In (c) one of the raw materials (RM_2) is heavier than the other and the finished product – so the factory is located nearer to RM_2.

Weber used the Material Index to discover where an industry would be located:

$$\text{Material Index} = \frac{\text{weight of raw materials}}{\text{weight of finished product}}$$

An industry with an index of over 1 will be located nearer the raw materials. An industry with an index of under 1 will be located nearer the market.
Example: In baking, 1 tonne of flour produces 2 tonnes of bread. Material Index is $1 \div 2 = 0.5$. So baking should be located near the market.

Criticisms of Weber's model:
- The model places too much importance upon transport costs
- The model assumes that transport costs increase with weight; this is not always the case – costs may increase with the bulkiness of the goods
- The model assumes that the least-cost location will also be the place where most profit can be made – this is not necessarily the case
- Labour, power or land costs may be more important than transport costs
- Government policy may provide grants and loans which improve the costs of more expensive locations

Figure B

In reality, many factors will affect a company's decision (Figure C). Of course, the people making the decisions are only human and they can make mistakes. There are many examples of factories located in less than ideal places. Once an area develops industries it tends to continue developing as more industries are attracted in because of those already there. Service and component industries develop. This is called the *multiplier effect* (Figure D). Some industrial areas gain a reputation for certain types of industry. They attract similar industries as a result. An example is the high technology and electronics industrial area in and around Cambridge, known as 'Silicon Fen' (see section 5.7). Of course, the multiplier effect can work in reverse: the closure of one factory can lead to the closure of others. Many inner city areas have ceased to be important industrial regions in recent years as factory after factory has closed.

In the late twentieth century most industries in developed countries are 'footloose', with few important locating factors. This is because:
- Electricity and water are available in most areas
- Improved transport has reduced the need to be close to supplies of raw materials.

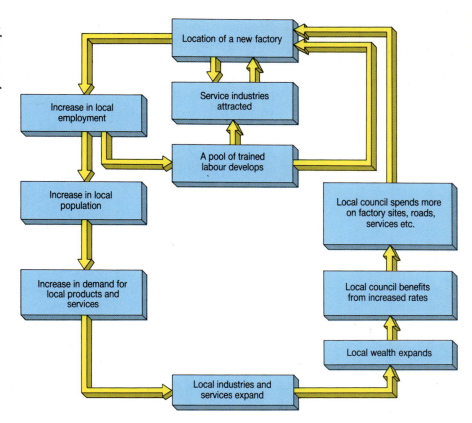

Many companies have chosen to move their factories from the older, congested inner city areas to more spacious locations in country towns. The quality of life available to the company's employees has become an important locating factor. It is no coincidence that Britain's fastest growing industrial areas are the rural regions such as East Anglia and the South-West.

Figure D The multiplier effect (simplified from Gunnar Myrdal's model)

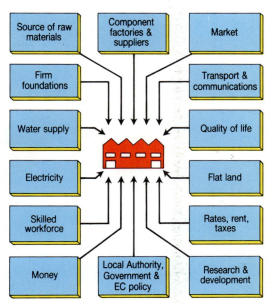

Figure C Factors affecting industrial location

QUESTIONS

4 Study Figure C. Make a list of the factors which can affect a company's decision to locate a factory under two headings PHYSICAL FACTORS and HUMAN FACTORS.

5 a) What is the 'multiplier effect'?
  b) How does the multiplier effect operate in reverse?

6 a) What is meant by 'footloose' industry?
  b) Why are more and more industries in developed countries footloose?

7 a) Outline Weber's theory of industrial location.
  b) What are (i) the least-cost location (ii) the material index?
  c) Draw a triangle to show the least-cost location for an industry whose product is twice as expensive to transport as its raw materials.
  d) How has Weber's theory of industrial location been criticized?

4.4 Industrial location 2

Recent studies of industrial location have highlighted the importance of the 'geography of the firm'. This means that locational decisions are made on the basis of a company's own requirements rather than external factors:

- A new company seeking a site for its first factory will be greatly affected by the managers' knowledge of the locations under consideration. They may choose a site which is known personally to them, perhaps near their homes.
- A company with several factories seeking a new site will base its decision upon the market for its products. The new factory will be built to fill gaps in the current locations of the company.
- A company which is controlled by the state will have to consider the interests of the nation and will be greatly influenced by the government.

For most companies, older factories dating back over 30 years or so tend to be located within urban areas. Such factories can only survive if they are modernized. However, the requirements of modern industry are such that it is often easier for a company to build a new factory on an undeveloped, or 'greenfield', site.

The geography of Ford Europe

Ford is a US-owned multi-national company. It was started by Henry Ford, an engineer. He built his first car in 1896 in a shed in his garden in Detroit. He set up his first car factory in this city in 1903. Ford cars were sold in Europe as well as the USA and Ford looked for a site to manufacture his cars in Europe. In 1911 he chose a site on the Trafford Park industrial estate beside the Manchester Docks. There were regular shipping services to the USA and easy

Figure A (top) Ford's UK car assembly plant at Dagenham

Figure B (bottom) Ford's UK car assembly plant at Halewood

Figure C (bottom right) The location of Ford Europe's factories

export routes throughout Europe. Britain was chosen since it was the major European market for Ford's cars at that time. It was an advantage that both British and American workforces spoke English.

The Trafford Park factory was not large enough to have the new assembly line production method introduced. In 1924 Ford looked for a new site. Dagenham in Essex was chosen. It was near London, the largest market for cars in Britain. The new factory was opened in 1931 on a 230 hectare site beside the River Thames. The factory has its own wharf through which materials are imported and finished cars exported. As demand for cars increased in Britain after the Second World War a new site was sought. There were labour shortages in Essex and the government's regional policy made it difficult for Ford to build a new factory outside the Development Areas. A site at Halewood near Liverpool was finally chosen and the new factory was opened in 1962.

Ford's British factories supplied the European market for several years, but Ford was soon seeking a site in the two major markets, Germany and France. The French government refused to allow the American company to build a factory because it was worried about the effect which Ford would have on the small French car makers. The Germans allowed a small factory to be opened in Berlin in 1925 but, like Trafford Park, this proved too small to be expanded. In 1931 a new factory was opened at Cologne beside the River Rhine.

Until 1962 Ford's European car factories were limited to just two. However the increasing wealth of the European people in the 1960s created a rapidly growing demand for cars. Ford opened new factories at Halewood, at Genk in Belgium (in 1963) and at Saarlouis in West Germany (in 1968).

In 1967 Ford Europe was established to oversee Ford operations throughout Europe. Ford Europe decided to limit production to only a few models which would be sold throughout Europe. This organizational change meant that Ford now adopted a Europe-wide view of its operations.

The concentration of the demand for cars in North-West Europe was reflected in the location of Ford's factories. However, during the late 1960s the demand for cars increased in southern Europe, especially in Spain, Italy and France. This demand was for smaller, cheaper cars. Spain offered an important market, but Spanish law restricted imports of cars built in the EC except at very high rates of tax. Ford chose a site in Valencia to build a new small car, the Fiesta. This plant allowed Ford to break into the Spanish market and was also a favourable location for exports to the rest of southern Europe, North Africa and the Middle East. Spanish wage levels were also lower than those in northern Europe and the trade unions were less strong.

Ford Europe employs 110 000 people in its assembly and component plants sited in six countries. Location decisions are now clearly based on the geography of the firm.

Figure D A Ford for the 1960s – Anglia

Figure E A Ford for the 1980s – Escort

QUESTIONS

1 a) What is meant by 'the geography of the firm'?
   b) How does the geography of the firm affect the following companies seeking a new factory site: (i) a new company (ii) an existing company with several factories (iii) a state-controlled company?

2 Why did Henry Ford locate his first car factory at Detroit?

3 a) Why was Trafford Park a suitable location for Ford's first European factory in 1911?
   b) Why was Trafford Park no longer suitable for car production in 1924?
   c) Explain why (i) Dagenham and (ii) Halewood were chosen as the site for Ford car factories.

4 What important change was made in 1967 which affected Ford's view of its European operations?

5 What were the locational advantages of Valencia for Ford?

6 If Ford decided to close one of its existing European car plants, what factors would they have to consider in choosing which location to close?

Unit 4 ASSESSMENT

A Japanese company, Lightning Electronics Ltd, wants to build a new factory in Britain. The factory will manufacture compact disc players for the European market. Lightning Electronics have a number of requirements for the location of their new factory:

- Easy access to an airport with a range of scheduled international flights;
- Easy access to a deepwater seaport;
- A 50 hectare site with room available for future expansion;
- Easy access to the motorway network;
- A readily available semi-skilled workforce;
- Good labour relations;
- A fully serviced site with roads, gas, electricity, water and telephones already provided;
- Government and/or local government assistance with finance;
- Other Japanese companies in the area;
- Easy access to attractive countryside;

Ten sites have been short-listed by Lightning Electronics' planners for consideration. The ten sites are shown on Figure A.

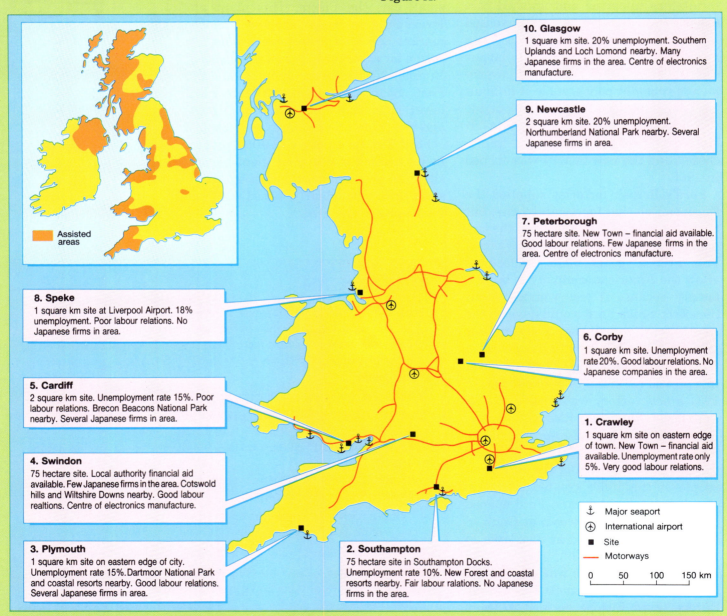

Figure A The ten possible sites for the Lightning Electronics factory

1. a) Consider the advantages and disadvantages of each site and fill in the matrix below by using the following points system:
   1 POINT for POOR
   2 POINTS for AVERAGE
   3 POINTS for GOOD
   −1 POINT for any disadvantage
   (If no information is given score 2 points)

Scoring matrix for factory sites

Requirement	Site									
	1	2	3	4	5	6	7	8	9	10
Access to airport										
Access to seaport										
Access to motorway network										
Size of site										
Available workforce										
Labour relations										
Fully serviced site										
Government/local authority assistance										
Other Japanese companies in the area										
Access to attractive countryside										

b) Calculate the total points score for each site. (20 marks)

c) List the leading three sites. Write down the advantages of each of the three sites and decide which site you think Lightning Electronics should choose. (10 marks)

2. a) Why do you think easy access to (i) an airport with scheduled international flights, (ii) a deepwater seaport and (iii) the motorway network was so important for Lightning Electronics? (6 marks)

   b) Why was it important for other Japanese companies to be in the area? (3 marks)

   c) Why was easy access to attractive countryside important? (3 marks)

3. What type of industry is compact disc manufacture?
   A. primary   B. secondary   C. tertiary   (1 mark)

4. a) What do the following terms used in industrial location mean?
   i) Raw materials location. (2 marks)
   ii) Market location. (2 marks)
   iii) Footloose. (2 marks)

   b) Which location applies to compact disc manufacturing? (1 mark)

TOTAL: 50 marks

Details for pupil profile sheet Unit 4

Knowledge and understanding

1. Industry
2. Primary, secondary, tertiary
3. Multi-national company
4. Factories
5. Industrial location, footloose industry
6. Weber's theory of industrial location
7. The multiplier effect
8. The geography of the firm
9. Greenfield site
10. Cycle of wealth creation

Skills

1. Drawing a flow diagram
2. Construct a simple industrial system diagram
3. Make locational decisions
4. Interpret a map
5. Drawing a Weberian locational triangle
6. Completing a matrix

Values

1. Awareness of the role of industry in wealth creation
2. Make reasoned and balanced judgements on industrial location

5.1 Oil refining

Unit 5: Key industries

Our modern world depends upon oil. All the items shown on the left are made from oil.

Crude oil arriving at the surface at an oil well is a mixture of liquids and gases. The oil has to be processed at an oil refinery to separate the various products from which so many familiar things are made.

Locating an oil refinery

Oil became big business early in this century. The first refineries were built near the oilfields, an example of resource location. The Middle East, Venezuela and the Caribbean became important centres of oil refining. Soon the increasing range of oil products made transport expensive; it was much cheaper to transport crude oil in large ships than to transport products in many smaller ships. As a result oil refineries were built in the developed countries, providing examples of market location.

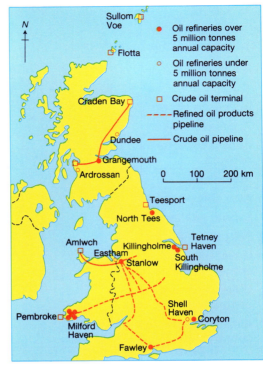

Figure B Oil refining in Britain

Britain's first major oil refinery was built at Llandarcy near Swansea in 1922. This has since closed but South Wales remains Britain's most impor-

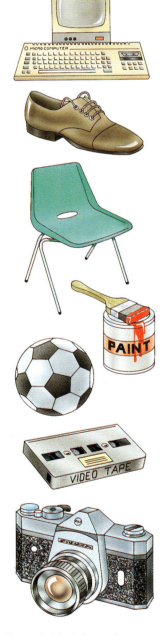

Figure A Made from oil

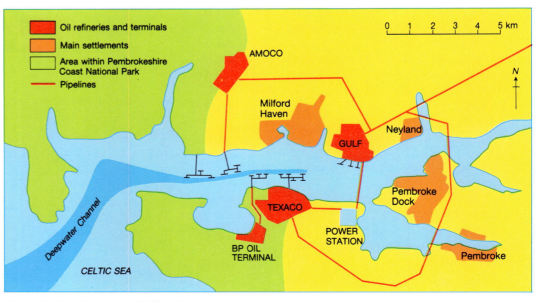

Figure C The oil industry of Milford Haven

tant oil refining centre. By 1974 there were four oil refineries and an oil terminal located around the shores of Milford Haven, 100 km west of Swansea. Milford Haven was a ria – a river valley drowned by rising sea waters at the end of the Ice Age. The natural deep water channel allows giant oil tankers of up to 280 000 tonnes to dock safely.

Other advantages of Milford Haven are the relatively flat sites, ample supplies of water (up to 24 million litres per hour are needed for cooling), and good road and rail communications. It is also well situated on the tanker route from the Middle East oilfields.

Texaco opened a refinery in Pembroke in 1964 which now has a capacity of nine million tonnes per year. Tankers moor at the refinery's five-berth jetty which has been built out to the deep-water channel. Crude oil is pumped from the ships to huge storage tanks before being refined. There are over 140 storage tanks on the 350 hectare site. Despite the great size and cost of the refinery only 450 people are employed. The refinery is a good example of a capital intensive industry.

Since the mid-1970s demand for oil has decreased due to rising prices and the economic recession. This has meant closure of 43 oil refineries in Western Europe between 1974 and 1987, eight of the closures in Britain.

One of the British refineries closed was the Esso refinery at Milford Haven. Closed in 1983, it has been dismantled and shipped out to Ajman in the United Arab Emirates. Several new refineries are being opened in Saudi Arabia, Kuwait and the United Arab Emirates, paid for by governments keen to expand their countries' industrial base. The new refineries can take advantage of local oil produced at costs far below North Sea oil. Resource location in oil refining is making a come-back.

Figure D Texaco's Pembroke refinery – deep water plus flat land

QUESTIONS

1 List ten things around you which are made from oil.

2 The table below shows the development of oil refining in the UK:

Year	1938	1950	1955	1965	1975	1980	1985
Number of refineries	8	13	15	18	22	18	14
Annual capacity (million tonnes)	2	11	30	72	150	122	88

a) Draw a line graph to illustrate the annual refinery capacity between 1938 and 1985.
b) Try to explain the trends shown by the graph.

3 Describe the location of Britain's oil refineries.

4 a) Draw a sketch map showing the location of the Texaco Pembroke oil refinery.
   b) Why is Milford Haven a good oil refinery location?
   c) Describe and explain the trends in the amount of crude oil handled at Milford Haven revealed in the table below:

Year	1960	1965	1970	1975	1980	1985
Crude oil handled (million tonnes)	3	22	42	45	40	21

5.2 The steel industry 1

Iron and steel in Britain is a *traditional* industry. These metals have been produced for centuries and have formed a vital part of the economy of several of Britain's major industrial regions. Today there are only five major steelworks left. The recent decline in British steel is just one more stage in a series of changes which have affected the industry.

Small beginnings – water power

Early iron making sites were strongly influenced by raw materials which cost a lot to transport. The iron was smelted in a furnace heated by charcoal and waterwheels powered the bellows and hammers. The best sites were therefore in forested areas, beside rivers where iron ore was found close to the surface. The two most important sites were the Forest of Dean in Gloucestershire and the Weald of Kent and Sussex.

The move to the coalfields

In 1709, a Shropshire ironmaster called Abraham Darby perfected the use of coke instead of charcoal to smelt iron at Coalbrookdale. Darby's son, also called Abraham, invented the blast furnace which made the coke burn fiercely. Limestone was added to the blast furnace to remove impurities from the iron. The steam engine, fuelled by coal, replaced the waterwheel. Eight tonnes of coal were needed to produce one tonne of iron. The best location for ironworks was therefore on coalfields where iron ore could be found.

By 1800 90 per cent of all Britain's iron was being produced from four coalfields: South Wales, Shropshire, the 'Black Country' of Staffordshire and the East Midlands.

The move to the coast

Steel is produced by passing oxygen over iron to remove impurities. Before 1850 it was difficult and expensive to

Figure A The decline of steelmaking in Britain

Year	1972	1985
Steel production (million tonnes)	25	15
Steel-workers (thousands)	301	77
Major steelworks	14	5

Figure B Changing location in the steel industry:
(*below*) small beginnings – water power
(*right*) the move to the coalfields
(*far right*) the move to the coast

make steel, so it was only used in small amounts. In 1856 Henry Bessemer discovered a cheap steel making process using his 'Bessemer Converter', but British ores were unsuitable for the process because they contained too much phosphorous. Foreign ore needed to be imported and British ores were running out anyway. This caused new steelworks to be built on the coast. Improvements in blast furnace design meant that only three tonnes of coal were needed to make one tonne of iron. This meant steelworks could be further from coal producing areas.

New steelmaking areas developed on Teesside and the coast of South Wales. But economic factors are not the only ones which determine the location of new steelworks. For example, in 1958 a company planned to build a new steelworks of six million tonnes capacity on the coast at Llanwern in South Wales. However, the government insisted that two separate three million tonne capacity works were built, one at Llanwern and the other at Ravenscraig, an inland site in central Scotland. The reason was to relieve the high unemployment in the Scottish coalfield area.

The invention of the Gilchrist-Thomas process of steelmaking in 1879 allowed phosphoric ores to be used. New steelworks developed at Corby and Scunthorpe.

Rationalization

In 1967 the British Steel Corporation was formed when private steel companies were nationalized (taken over by the government). The BSC decided that the cheapest way to produce steel was in large *integrated* works where iron and steel manufacture took place at the one site.

By 1980 only 1 tonne of coal was needed to produce 1 tonne of steel, and 80 per cent of the iron ore used in Britain was imported. All the coalfield based steelworks, with the exception of Ravenscraig, had closed by 1980. Even Ravenscraig no longer uses local coal.

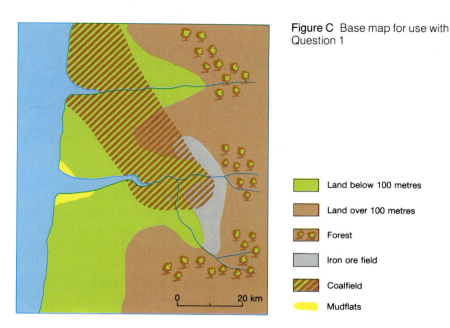

Figure C Base map for use with Question 1

- Land below 100 metres
- Land over 100 metres
- Forest
- Iron ore field
- Coalfield
- Mudflats

QUESTIONS

1 Make a large copy of Figure C.
   a) Choose three suitable sites for small seventeenth century ironworks and mark them on the map. Label on the map the raw materials and power source.
   b) Choose two suitable sites for early nineteenth century ironworks. Label the raw materials and power source.
   c) Choose the best site for a twentieth century steelworks. Label the raw materials.
   d) Give reasons why you chose each site.

2 The table below shows British steel production:

Year	1960	1965	1970	1975	1980	1985
Production (million tonnes)	22.4	27.4	26.3	22.3	11.3	15.1

   a) Draw a line graph to illustrate these statistics.
   b) Describe and try to explain the pattern shown by the graph.

3 The table below shows the amount of coal needed to produce one tonne of iron in Britain:

Year	1750	1840	1875	1935	1985
Coal needed (tonnes)	8.0	3.5	2.3	1.7	0.5

   a) Draw a bar graph to illustrate these statistics.
   b) How do these figures help to explain the locational changes in the British steel industry between 1750 and 1985?
   c) What do you understand by 'social factors' in industrial location? How have social factors affected the location of the British steel industry?

4 You are a member of the Public Relations department of the British Steel Corporation. You have been asked to produce an A4 pamphlet which briefly describes the history of the iron and steel industry in Britain and accounts for the location of the industry today. Use the information on these pages, plus anything else you may have. Remember to include maps.

5.3 The steel industry 2

As Figure A shows, the British steel industry is now a shadow of its former self. Its collapse was due to:

- an over-ambitious development programme committed BSC to paying very high interest charges;
- a drop in demand for steel because of the economic recession;
- poor industrial relations;
- a very poor productivity record (in 1974 only 9.5 tonnes of steel were produced per employee per month in Britain compared to 19.2 in West Germany and 20.7 in Italy);
- increased foreign competition.

Another important factor is that Britain's steel industry is now an integral part of the EC steel industry and subject to EC quotas. The EC Commission regularly called for cuts in British steel-making capacity. By the late 1980s Britain's steel industry was leaner and more competitive, but its future is tied in with the future of the EC industry as a whole.

Figure A The major British steelworks today

Steelmaking at Port Talbot

Port Talbot lies on the coast of South Wales, 16 kilometres south-east of Swansea. Docks were first opened here in 1837. In 1901 the first steelworks was built beside the docks, and in 1916 another was built at Margam. In the early 1950s an integrated iron and steelworks, the Abbey works, was built at Margam. By the early 1960s Port Talbot boasted the largest steelworks in Europe. In 1967 Port Talbot was selected as one of the 'Big Five' steelworks

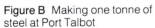
Figure B Making one tonne of steel at Port Talbot

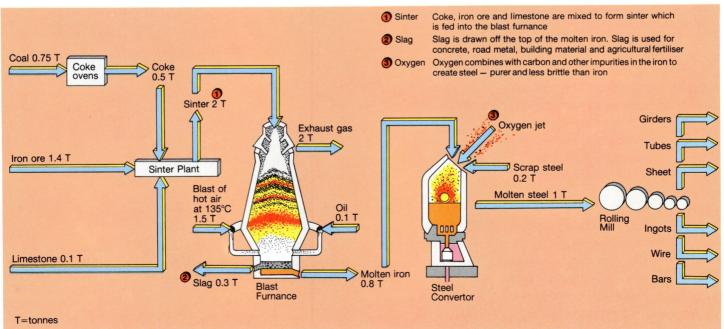

Figure C Port Talbot – an ideal location for a steelworks?

where future developments would be concentrated.

Why was Port Talbot such a good site for a steelworks? Figure C shows some of the major reasons. An important further reason is that the British government was keen to provide work in an area where mining jobs were declining.

Port Talbot's main product is sheet steel which is used in the motor industry, household goods such as washing machines and the construction industry. Port Talbot also makes all the steel used in the British tinplate industry. The works has an annual capacity of three million tonnes of steel a year. This is now small by world standards, for example the Taranto steelworks in Italy has a capacity of ten million tonnes per year.

Although Port Talbot remains a vital part of Britain's steel industry, the works has had to endure job losses. The introduction of new automated equipment has meant that the workforce at Port Talbot has dropped from 12 500 in 1980 to 4 750 by 1986.

QUESTIONS

1 Where is Port Talbot?

2 Study the table below:

The changing population of Port Talbot

Year	1911	1921	1931	1951	1961	1971	1981
Population (thousands)	32	40	41	44	50	51	47

   a) Draw a line graph to illustrate these statistics.
   b) Describe and explain the pattern revealed by the graph.

3 a) What is the annual capacity of Port Talbot steelworks?
   b) How many people work there?
   c) What is the main product of the steelworks? Which industries use the product?

4 Study Figure B. Copy and complete the flow chart below:

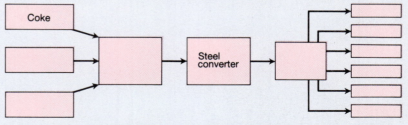

5 Explain why Port Talbot is a suitable location for an integrated steelworks.

5.4 The motor industry

The car industry is never far from the headlines. And what an industry it is – employing tens of millions of people throughout the world. In 1986 30 million cars were sold across the world.

This important industry is itself a product of the twentieth century. In the early days only the rich could afford to buy cars. Early cars were called 'horseless carriages' and indeed many of them looked like carriages and coaches. The cars were made by hand by skilled craftsmen. This was a slow process. As a result the cars were expensive.

Mass production

The real breakthrough in the car industry was when cars became cheaper so that more people could afford them. This was largely thanks to one man, Henry Ford. He changed the face of the car industry from a few skilled craftsmen working in small workshops to thousands of people working in large factories.

Henry Ford developed the method of 'mass production'. This divided the assembly of a car into many separate jobs each of which was simple enough for one person to do. A car was built on an 'assembly line' which was a conveyor carrying the car through the factory. Parts were added to the car as it moved along the conveyor.

Ford's assembly line methods changed the shape of factories. The traditional tall building was replaced by a long, large, single-storey building. A car assembly plant had several important locational requirements:

- a large area of flat land;
- a large labour force nearby;
- good transport links in order to bring together the many components and deliver the finished cars.

The British car industry

The early car factories in Britain grew out of the bicycle and coach building trades. The Midlands and Scotland with their long tradition of engineering were important locations. London and the South-East were important as the largest market for cars.

By the 1920s only the Midlands and the South-East remained important centres of the motor industry. Sixty per cent of total production was in the Midlands, especially Coventry and Birmingham. In the South-East the main centres were Dagenham, Oxford and Luton.

In the 1950s and 1960s the car industry grew rapidly as people became wealthier. Companies wanted to expand their factories in the Midlands and South-East but the government forced them to open new factories in the Development Areas. Ford went to Halewood near Liverpool, Vauxhall to Ellesmere Port, Peugeot Talbot to Linwood in Scotland and the Rover Group to Speke, Liverpool.

By 1970 over half a million people worked in the car industry and nearly two million cars a year were built. By 1986 these figures had been halved. More cars than ever are being sold in Britain, but most of them are now foreign imports. Several car factories have closed (Figure B).

In the late 1980s British car production increased again, but this was due to the US multi-nationals, Ford and General Motors, building more cars in

COMFORT AND SPEED!
European Car of the Year!
New Design Breakthrough!
Power with Economy!
0 to 60 in 7 seconds!

Figure A Early days of mass production – a Ford assembly line from the 1920s

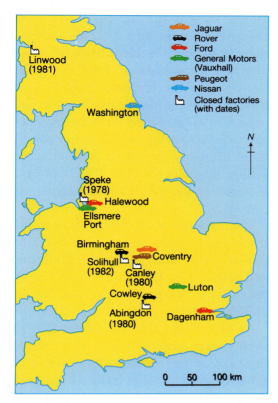

Figure B Car assembly factories in the UK

Britain because of the low value of the pound which made production in Britain cheaper than in some other European countries with stronger currencies.

Reasons for the decline of the British motor industry
- British cars and production gained a reputation for being unreliable
- British car designs lagged behind
- British car factories were slow to introduce new technology (robots)
- British car companies were too slow to respond to foreign competition
- Japanese cars proved cheap and reliable
- The American multi-national companies which owned two of Britain's four large car companies (Ford and Vauxhall) began to import many cars from their European factories and invested more money overseas
- British car makers lost a lot of money and were forced to close several factories

What's it like on the line?
An interview with a car worker

There isn't much time to talk on the line. The speed of the conveyor is worked out to ensure the maximum effort from all concerned... We don't work in seconds, they're too long. Instead we use 'centi-minutes', one-hundredths of a minute... You've got to know what you're doing... If you fumble or drop something you have to be quick or you put everybody in trouble. Its hard work, bent over the engine compartment and walking slowly backwards to avoid being run over as the line moves... This is a hard job. Its boring and there's a lot of pressure. The pay's all right, but it isn't marvellous. We earn it. At 4.15 we leave this place as fast as we can. Each night as I try to sleep I count cars, not sheep!

QUESTIONS

1 Why were early motor cars expensive?

2 Copy the diagram below and, in your own words, say what mass production means.

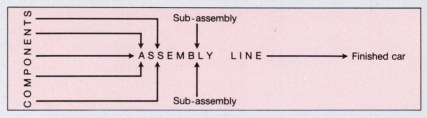

3 List the locational requirements of a car assembly plant.

4 Study the table below:

Car production in Britain

Year	1960	1965	1970	1975	1980	1985	1990
Cars built (in millions)	1.0	1.7	1.9	1.3	0.9	1.0	1.3

a) Draw a bar graph to illustrate these statistics.
b) Explain the pattern shown by the graph.

5 How and why has the location of the motor industry in Britain changed during the twentieth century?

6 The table below shows car production in 1965 and 1990:

Worldwide car production (millions)

Country	1965	1990
USA	9.3	6.3
West Germany	2.7	4.7
UK	1.7	1.3
France	1.4	3.3
Italy	1.1	2.3
Canada	0.7	1.1
Japan	0.7	9.9
Spain	0.1	1.7

a) Copy the table in rank order for 1990.
b) Which countries have (i) moved down and (ii) moved up in rank order, and by how much?
c) How does the table help to explain the decline in the British car industry?

5.5 A vehicle factory

Figure A shows the vast Austin Rover car factory at Cowley, Oxford. Oxford is one of the cradles of the British motor industry. Cars have been made there for over seventy years.

The Cowley car factory was started by William Morris. When he was three years old his family moved to Oxford, then simply a small university city of 40 000 people. Morris was interested in transport. In 1892 he made his first bicycle. He bought a small workshop where he built and repaired bicycles. As business grew he rented a disused schoolroom in Cowley. In 1912 he made his first motor car at Cowley in a new factory. William Morris is a good example of an 'entrepreneur', a person who owns a business, raises money and takes risks to make the business grow.

Morris was successful. By 1913 Morris Motors employed 300 people. At that time the car industry was concentrated in London and the Midlands. Oxford was a good location because it was halfway between the two places. Workshops and factories in Birmingham and Coventry supplied car parts and London was where most customers for cars lived. In these early days Morris bought his car parts from the cheapest sources and sold his cars as cheaply as possible. He introduced mass production methods in 1921. By 1925 Cowley was the largest car factory in Europe. Morris Motors built up a fortune. In 1927 a second large factory was opened at Cowley when the Pressed Steel company moved in to supply car bodies to Morris. By 1938 Morris Motors employed 10 000 people at Cowley.

The expansion of Morris Motors attracted thousands of people to move to Oxford, particularly from the Midlands and South-West England. Within thirty years the city's population doubled, to 81 000 by 1931.

At its height in the 1970s 27 000 people were employed at Cowley building cars or car components. Following the cutbacks of the later 1970s and early 1980s employment at Cowley fell to 11 500 by 1987. Cowley builds three models of car, the Austin Maestro, Austin Montego and Rover 800. Over 200 000 cars are built each year. The introduction of automated methods, including computer-controlled robots, has increased the efficiency and quality of

Figure A Austin Rover's Cowley assembly plant is one of Britain's largest factories

the car production. It has also reduced the labour requirements. This can be illustrated by considering the number of people required to prepare and install the windscreens in the cars on the assembly line. The Maestro line, dating from 1982, needs twenty people. The tasks are all performed by hand. The Montego line, dating from 1984, uses an early robot to fit the windscreens. Only twelve people are needed. The Rover 800 line, dating from 1986, uses a more efficient robotic system and requires only four people!

Cowley is one of only two assembly plants in the Austin Rover section of the Rover Group, the other is at Longbridge in Birmingham. The Cowley factory receives the majority of its components from within a 100 kilometre radius, especially important are Swindon from where the car bodies are obtained, the West Midlands and Greater London. It is still important to be close to suppliers, not just to keep transport costs low, but also so that points of planning and research can be discussed quickly. Today's motor industry is international, however, and Cowley obtains gearboxes from Volkswagen in West Germany, and other components from Japan.

Austin Rover Cowley is big business:
- Cowley's cars sell for a total of £1 500 million a year
- 25 per cent of the cars built at Cowley are exported, earning £375 million in foreign currency
- 11 500 workers are paid over £100 million a year in wages
- Over £200 million is paid in car tax to the government
- £34 million is paid for local services, heating and power
- £26 million is paid to suppliers of services and components outside the local area
- £15 million is paid to local contractors who clean and maintain the factories
- £4 million is paid in rates to local councils

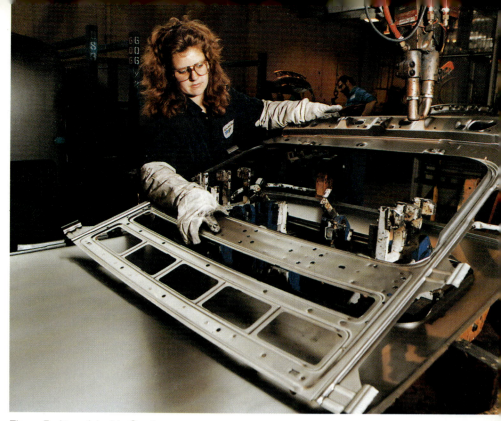

Figure B At work inside Cowley

QUESTIONS

1 Where is Cowley?
2 When were the first motor cars built at Cowley?
3 a) Explain in your own words what the term 'entrepreneur' means.
   b) What evidence is there that William Morris was an entrepreneur?
4 Study the table below:

The population of Oxford

Year	Population (thousands)
1901	49
1911	56
1921	67
1931	81
1939 (estimate)	96
1951	99
1961	106
1971	109
1981	99

a) Draw a line graph to show these statistics.
b) Describe and explain the shape of the graph.
5 Explain in your own words why Cowley was a suitable site for a car factory.
6 What contribution does Austin Rover Cowley make to (a) the local and (b) the national economy?

5.6 The defence industry

The defence industry is one of the largest industries in Britain. Almost a million and a half people, including those in the armed forces, are employed in the industry.

The defence industries include:
- warship building;
- military aircraft, helicopters and missiles;
- tanks and military vehicles;
- ammunition and weapons (ordnance);
- computer, radar and electronics systems;
- military support services;
- research and development.

Figure B shows the location of two of the most important defence industries, aerospace and warships. The location of these industries reflect two factors. Firstly, those areas with a tradition of heavy engineering which provide the skilled workforce and support structure needed. Secondly, those locations in the south of England which have easy access to government departments, finance and high technology research centres.

The aerospace industry employs over 200 000 people. The bulk of them are employed in defence work. 80 per cent of British Aerospace's business is in military products. One of the largest military programmes is the Tornado multi-role combat aircraft. By 1987 933 Tornadoes had been ordered by the air

Figure A Products of the defence industry: a Tornado aircraft launching a sky flash missile (*below*), a Chieftain tank (*below right*), HMS *Turbulent*, a Trafalgar-class submarine (*bottom right*), the infantryman is wearing protective clothing and is armed with a combat rifle, and behind him is a Lynx helicopter (*bottom left*)

forces of Britain, West Germany, Italy, Saudi Arabia and Oman. The swing-wing Tornado is built by Panavia, a consortium of British, West German and Italian companies in which British Aerospace has a 42.5 per cent interest. British Aerospace builds the forward and rear fuselage and the tail of the Tornado, and is responsible for the final assembly of all aircraft delivered to the Royal Air Force. Major assemblies for the Tornado are manufactured at Prestwick, Preston, Warton and Samlesbury. Components are made at Bristol and Hurn. Production of the Tornado started in 1980 and is scheduled to continue until 1992. Such long production runs of military aircraft are only possible because of the collaboration between several countries. The very high cost of military aircraft makes it difficult for a European country to afford to work alone.

Defence industries have a major role in the British economy:
- Over 6 per cent of the country's national income is spent on defence
- Over 8 per cent of the nation's workforce is employed in defence industries
- Over half of Britain's research scientists are employed in defence research
- Weapons make up 13 per cent of total manufacturing production
- Exports of military equipment make up 11 per cent of total exports.

Many people criticize the amount of money spent on defence. They point out that the money could be better spent on hospitals, schools, pensions, foreign aid etc. It is said that six month's worth of the world's military spending would be enough to provide clean and reliable water supplies for all the world's population. A single Tornado fighter aircraft costs more than a new hospital.

Figure B The location of military aerospace factories and warship yards

QUESTIONS

1 Name five defence industries.
2 Study the table below:

Employment in the defence industries

Type of employment	Workforce
Armed forces	340 000
Ministry of Defence civilian workers	225 000
Arms manufacturers	410 000
Suppliers and services	360 000
Total	1 335 000

  a) Draw a bar graph to illustrate these statistics.
  b) Name the three armed forces.
3 Describe the importance of the defence industries to the British economy.
4 a) On an outline map of Britain show the factories involved in the Tornado aircraft programme.
  b) Name the two countries with which British Aerospace collaborates in the production of the Tornado.
  c) Why was it necessary for British Aerospace to seek partners in the Tornado programme?
5 'Many people criticize the amount of money spent on defence.'
  a) Why do these people criticize the amount?
  b) Why is so much money spent on defence?
  c) Do you think that too much money is spent on defence? Give reasons for your answer.

5.7 High-tech industry

The 1980s were harsh times for many of Britain's traditional industries. Steel, coal, chemicals, shipbuilding, heavy engineering, car assembly... all these industries, and many more, declined rapidly. The old industrial regions like North-East England, Merseyside, South Wales and the West Midlands became areas of factory closures and high unemployment.

Despite the general decline in manufacturing, there have been some areas and some manufacturing industries which have grown during the 1980s. Most of them are the so-called 'sunrise' industries marking a new dawn in high-technology industry.

So what does high-technology really mean? There is no single definition, but most high-tech industries involve the development or assembly of micro-electronics and computers. High-technology industry is footloose, not being tied to any single source of materials. However, some of the industry's requirements have favoured certain locations:

- a highly skilled workforce is needed;
- it is necessary to keep in touch with scientific advances;
- the highly paid workforce demands an attractive environment in which to work and live.

The result of these factors is that high-technology industry has tended to steer clear of the traditional industrial areas and the inner cities. A typical location for high-technology industry is shown in Figure A – on a 'greenfield' site on the edge of a country town, near a motorway junction and a university. Three areas have attracted large numbers of high-technology jobs:

1. The 'Western Corridor' following the M4 motorway from West London to Bristol
2. 'Silicon Glen' in central Scotland
3. 'Silicon Fen' in and around Cambridge.

The Cambridge Science Park

One of the greatest single high-technology sites is the Cambridge Science Park. The Science Park was opened in 1973 on 50 hectares of derelict land in north Cambridge. Ready-built factories and laboratories were made available. The land was owned by one of the colleges of Cambridge University and the Science Park has had close links with the University from the start. This has given access to some of Britain's top scientific brains working at the university.

Easy access to the M11 motorway has increased the site's attractions for high-technology industry. Two thousand people are employed there in nearly 70 companies. The largest employs just over 300, but half the companies have under 20 people. Most of the companies are manufacturing computers, telecommunications and precision instruments. The BBC micro-computer was developed and built here, for example. There are an increasing number of companies involved in *bio-technology* on the Science Park. These include among their products drugs and medical instruments. There are several companies concentrating on research and development, notably in lasers. Many of the

Figure A High-tech industrial estate beside the M5 motorway in Avon

Figure B (*left*) The entrance to the Cambridge Science Park

Figure C (*below left*) Inside the NAPP bio-technology plant on the Cambridge Science Park

research workers on the Science Park are employed at the University laboratories on a part-time basis.

The success of the Cambridge Science Park has encouraged other universities – by 1987 there were 26 science parks linked with British universities. Four hundred and twenty companies were based on these science parks.

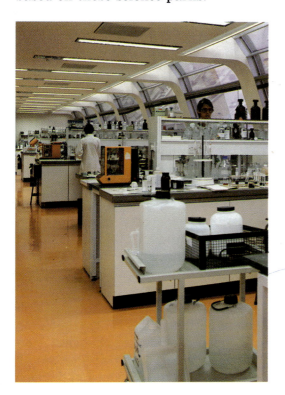

QUESTIONS

1 a) What does 'high-tech industry' mean?
  b) List five examples of high-tech industry's products.
  c) What factors affect the location of high-tech industry?

2 On an outline map of Britain show the three areas which have attracted large numbers of high-technology jobs.

3 a) What do you think the terms 'sunrise' and 'sunset' industry mean?
  b) Give examples of both types of industry.

4 a) What is the Cambridge Science Park?
  b) Describe the development of the Park.

5 The area in and around Cambridge is known as Silicon Fen because of the large number of high-tech industries there. Study the table below:

High-tech industry in Silicon Fen

Type of industry	Percentage of companies
Computer software	25
Electronics	19
Precision instruments	17
Computer hardware	13
Research	8
Bio-technology	7
Others	11

  a) Draw a proportional bar to show this information.
  b) What is meant by computer 'software' and computer 'hardware'?
  c) Why have so many high-technology companies been attracted to Cambridge?

6 By 1987 there were 26 university-linked science parks. They were located at the following sites:
  Aberdeen, Aberystwyth, Aston (Birmingham), Bath, Belfast, Bradford, Brunel (Uxbridge), Cambridge, Durham, East Anglia (Norwich), Essex (Colchester), Heriot Watt (Edinburgh), Hull, Keele (Newcastle-under-Lyme), Kent (Canterbury), Leeds, Loughborough, Manchester, Nottingham, Southampton, St. Andrews, Stirling, Strathclyde (Glasgow), Surrey (Guildford), Swansea, Warwick (Kenilworth).
  a) Mark the location of these Science Parks on the outline map of Britain which you used for question 2.
  b) What do you think are the advantages for (i) industry and (ii) the university of university-linked science parks?

7 Can you think of any problems which have been caused by the replacement of traditional industries by high-tech industries?

5.8 Offices

Telex machines, telephones, typewriters, word processors, daisywheel printers, photocopiers, filing cabinets and meeting rooms. You will find them all in a modern office. Who owns offices? What happens in them? Where are they?

Offices are needed by all major manufacturing companies. What other organizations need offices? Banks, building societies, insurance companies, travel operators, government departments, electricity and gas boards ... you can probably add to this list. Much of the business of a gas board such as Southern Gas is local. Large towns will have gas offices. The business of a whole gas region will be organized from a regional office in a city. All the gas boards in the country will be co-ordinated by the London headquarters office of British Gas.

You can see that offices need to be in a central place. They serve a local, regional, national or even international market. An accessible location is needed so that people can travel to the office, this includes office workers and visitors. The town or city centre has always been attractive for offices because of its accessibility and because of the contacts, or *linkages*, which develop between offices there. In the centre of Manchester (Figure A) you can see office blocks dominating the skyline.

Office blocks are often high-rise buildings. The company has to pay rents and rates on the land which its offices occupy. Land costs are greatest in the city centre (Figure B). Prices are raised because of the advantages of locating in the centre. To get the most from the land it is essential to build high. The more competition there is for land, the higher will be the buildings (subject to any planning limits).

City centres are the traditional location for offices. In recent years this has changed. Many offices are now being built in outer urban areas where land costs are lower, where there is less congestion and where the surroundings are more pleasant. Many companies have moved their head offices out of London to sites in New Towns and Expanded Towns or in the provinces.

'Business Parks' have been built throughout the country, but especially in South-East England. Most Business Parks are on out-of-town sites, with easy access to motorways or main roads. They feature landscaped sites and large car parks, especially attractive as office workers increasingly travel to work by car. The offices on such sites are usually only a few floors high and of the most modern design. All the new electronic and telecommunication equipment needs extensive wiring which has to be placed in raised floors or large ceiling spaces. It is very expensive to convert pre-1980 offices to cater for the requirements of the computerized office. Many 1960s and 1970s city centre offices now stand empty; customers prefer to buy new offices in the out-of-town locations.

Central London remains Britain's most important office centre, but even in London there are changes. New offices are being built on the South Bank of the River Thames at London

Figure A Manchester city centre is ringed by office blocks

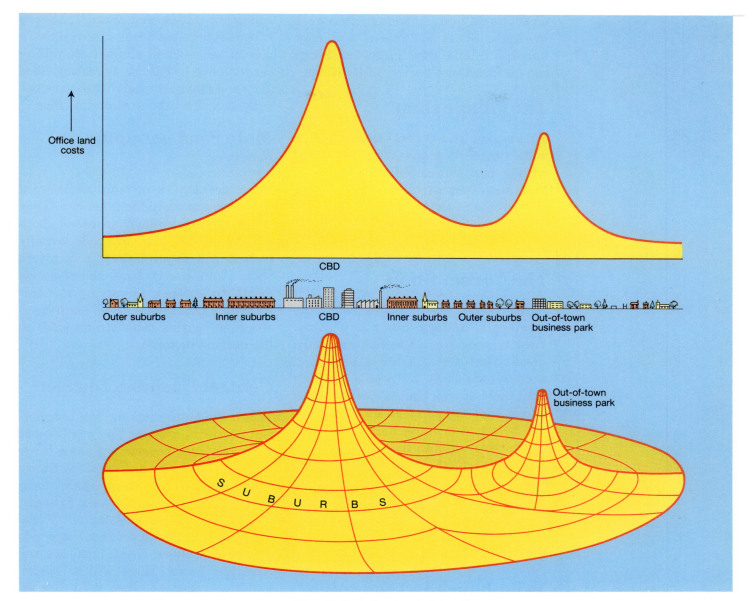

Figure B Office land costs in the city

Bridge City. Seven thousand office jobs will be provided there in a range of offices. Even larger developments are taking place in the East End of London. The Canary Wharf scheme at the old West India Docks plans to provide over 40 000 office jobs, mainly in insurance and finance. Road and rail developments will improve the accessibility of the docklands and the new London City Airport provides flights to major British and European cities. Land costs in the docklands are only a fifth of the costs in central London. It is thought that many companies will move their offices from central London to the docklands.

QUESTIONS

1 Name ten organizations with offices in your nearest town.
2 Why do offices need to be in a central place?
3 Why are office blocks often high-rise buildings?
4 Why are many new offices being built in out-of-town locations?
5 You work for the Employment section of a New Town Authority. Your authority is anxious to attract new office development to the town. Design an advertisement to be placed in the *Financial Times* newspaper aimed at attracting office employers and making them aware of the advantages of locating at your New Town. You might also like to point out on your advertisement some of the disadvantages that offices in London face.

5.9 Retailing

Over two million people in Britain work in shops. Shops are one of the most important land uses in towns. Shops can be found in a variety of locations.

The village shop

This is usually a general store selling a wide range of goods, often combined with a post office. Villages may lose their shop because of competition from nearby town shops which sell goods more cheaply because they have higher sales.

The Corner Shop

Corner shops were a feature of the nineteenth century inner city areas. They are similar in function to village shops. They serve a few streets and were visited daily by people walking from their nearby homes. Corner shops sold a wide range of goods. They can still be found in those inner city areas which have not been redeveloped. However, many have closed down because they cannot compete with supermarket prices. This is a pity because corner shops provide a valuable service, especially for those without cars and the elderly.

Neighbourhood shopping centres

These shopping centres serve large housing estates in the suburbs of towns. They are often in a parade of shops such as that shown in Figure A. Even the smaller parades will usually have a range of shops including a newsagent, a post office, a small chain store selling convenience goods, a takeaway food shop and maybe a specialist shop or two such as a chemists or electrical shop.

Main road shopping centres

These develop along main roads or at major crossroads in the inner city. They often contain twenty or more shops selling a wide range of goods, usually including a supermarket, a furniture shop, a DIY store, a bank and an estate agent. In addition to serving the surrounding inner city area, main road shopping centres benefit from sales to the passing motorist.

Central Business District

This is the main shopping and commercial centre in a town. There will be at least one large department store, large supermarkets such as Tesco, Sainsbury and Fine Fare, other large chain stores such as Woolworths, Marks & Spencer, Boots, Littlewoods and British Home Stores and many specialist shops selling clothes, shoes, books, furniture and consumer goods. There will be banks, building societies, insurance offices, estate agents and solicitors. There will be many service functions such as hairdressers, cafes, restaurants and travel agents. The CBD is the most accessible shopping centre in a town and may be crowded and congested. Land in the CBD is very expensive. Only the bigger and wealthier shops can afford to locate there. Large covered shopping precincts, like the Arndale Centre in Manchester, are common in larger CBDs.

Out-of-town shopping centres

These are a recent development. They are located on the outskirts of large towns and cities near major roads. The

Figure A A neighbourhood shopping parade – Rose Hill, Oxford

centres usually feature one very large shop called a superstore or *hypermarket* which provides a very wide range of goods. There will be other shops and services in the centre as well, often including a bank, a newsagent and a cafe. There is usually a petrol station and there may be large discount warehouses selling electrical goods, furniture, carpets, DIY etc. Figure C shows the Weston Favell Centre at Northampton. These out-of-town centres are designed to attract motorists from a wide area. They have free car parks and offer easier, less congested shopping than the CBD.

The size of out-of-town shopping centres has increased rapidly in recent years. The largest in the UK is the Metrocentre at Gateshead. It contains 130 shops including a Marks & Spencer superstore and a Carrefour hypermarket. Metrocentre provides an example of the trend towards combining retailing with other functions in an integrated development. Metrocentre includes a business park, office complexes, cinema, funfair and hotel.

In many US cities the CBD is no longer the most important shopping centre. Out-of-town centres have taken over. Many shopowners in British CBDs have become worried that the same could happen here.

Figure B Manchester's Central Business District

Figure C An out-of-town shoppping centre – Weston Favell, Northampton

QUESTIONS

1. a) What is a corner shop?
   b) Why have many corner shops closed?
   c) Why do corner shops provide a valuable service?
2. a) Describe the shopping centre shown in Figure A.
   b) Where would you expect to find this type of shopping centre?
3. a) What is the CBD?
   b) What types of shops and services would you expect to find in the CBD?
   c) Why is land very expensive in the CBD?
4. a) You own a small supermarket in the CBD of the town of Goodbury. You are dismayed to learn of a plan to build an out-of-town shopping centre. Write a letter to the local newspaper, the 'Goodbury Guardian', which explains the reasons why you oppose the plan.
   b) Now change roles. You are a director of Mega Markets plc which plans to open the out-of-town shopping centre at Goodbury. Write a letter which replies to the points made in the first letter and which makes the advantages of your plan clear to the 'Goodbury Guardian' readers.

Unit 5 ASSESSMENT

In the following questions five possible answers are given. Choose the best answer in each case.

1. Which one of these factors is not a reason for the present location of a steelworks at Port Talbot, South Wales?
   A. A deepwater harbour.
   B. A large flat site on the coastal plain.
   C. Blackband iron ore is available locally.
   D. A large pool of skilled labour in the area.
   E. Good motorway and rail links with the Midlands and South-East of England. (1 mark)

2. The map (Figure A) shows the present location of which industry in Britain?

   A. Iron and steelworks.
   B. Motor vehicle assembly plants.
   C. Warship yards.
   D. Oil refineries.
   E. Military aerospace factories. (1 mark)

Figure A

3. An assembly industry is one which
   A. makes parts for assembly elsewhere.
   B. distributes parts to other firms.
   C. uses robots and assembly lines.
   D. makes kits for export.
   E. assembles many parts into a finished product. (1 mark)

4. Which of the following is NOT an example of a 'high-tech' industry?
   A. Electronics.
   B. Computers.
   C. Food processing.
   D. Telecommunications.
   E. Precision instruments. (1 mark)

5. Which of the following would you expect to find in the Central Business District of a city?
   A. Assembly industries.
   B. Office blocks and shops.
   C. Heavy industry.
   D. Business parks.
   E. Component factories. (1 mark)

6. Study the table below:

The British steel industry

Year	Steel production (million tonnes)	Steelworkers (thousands)	Major steelworks
1960	22	350	33
1965	27	320	24
1970	26	310	17
1975	22	300	12
1980	11	220	6
1985	15	80	5

a) Draw a bar graph to show the figures for steelworkers. (8 marks)
b) Calculate the percentage change in steel production, steelworkers and major steelworks between 1960 and 1985. (3 marks)
c) Comment on what these percentage changes reveal. (3 marks)
d) In 1960 62.85 tonnes of steel were produced per steelworker. Calculate the figure for 1985. What does this calculation reveal? (4 marks)
e) Name four towns whose steelworks closed between 1960 and 1985. (4 marks)
f) What effect do you think the closure of a major steelworks has on a town? (5 marks)
g) Imagine that you are an officer of the British Steel Corporation. Write a letter to the mayor of a town justifying the closure of a steelworks in the mayor's town. (7 marks)
h) Imagine that you are an official of the steelworker's trade union. Write a letter to the BSC commenting on the plans to close a major steelworks. (7 marks)

7. Study the table below:

Bases of UK's thousand largest company's headquarters

Region	Number of company headquarters
Greater London	458
South-East	165
East Anglia	16
South-West	25
Wales	6
West Midlands	76
East Midlands	41
North-West	66
Yorkshire & Humberside	74
North	15
Scotland	54
Northern Ireland	4
TOTAL	1000

Figure B Regions of the UK

a) Make a copy of the outline map of the UK (Figure B) and shade in the regions as a choropleth map using the following divisions:
0–24; 25–74; 75–149; 150–299; over 300   (8 marks).
b) What percentage of the hedquarters are located in Greater London and the South East?   (1 mark)
c) What percentage of the headquarters are located in Wales, Scotland and Northern Ireland?   (1 mark)
d) Describe and explain the pattern shown by the map.   (6 marks)

8 Figure C shows the location of shopping centres in a town.
a) How many shopping centres have
(i) 1–9 shops (ii) 10–19 shops (iii) 20–50 shops
(iv) over 50 shops?   (4 marks)
b) Draw a bar graph to show the numbers in each group.   (5 marks)
c) Why have out-of-town shopping centres been built in recent years?   (4 marks)

Details for pupil profile sheet Unit 5

Knowledge and understanding
1 Oil refining
2 Traditional industry
3 Integrated steelworks
4 Nationalised industry
5 Mass production
6 Assembly line method
7 Economies of scale
8 Rank order
9 High-tech industry, bio-technology
10 Western Corridor, Silicon Glen, Silicon Fen

Skills
1 Drawing a line graph
2 Drawing a sketch map
3 Labelling a map
4 Interpreting statistical information from a table
5 Decision making, role play
6 Producing a publicity pamphlet
7 Drawing a bar graph
8 Interpreting a flow diagram
9 Copying a table in rank order
10 Interpreting an aerial photograph

Values
1 Empathy with a worker on an assembly line
2 Awareness of conflicting views on defence spending
3 Awareness of contrasting attitudes to progress

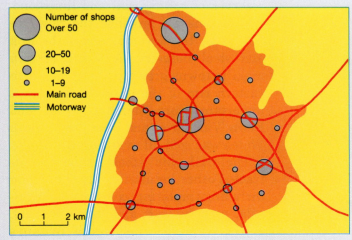

Figure C

TOTAL: 75 marks

6.1 South Wales 1

Unit 6: Industrial regions

Before 1800 South Wales was a sparsely populated farming region. Much of the area was hilly. Its attractive scenery was largely a result of the Ice Age. Glaciers had cut deep valleys southwards from an ice cap in the Brecon Beacons. The valley floors were thickly forested and impenetrable. However, the basis for the growth of industry lay beneath the ground: iron ore, limestone, and, above all, coal.

The coal rush

After 1800 the demand for coal rapidly increased as Britain's new industries used steam engines fuelled by coal. A 'coal rush' began. Hundreds of coal mines were sunk beneath the Welsh Valleys in a desperate race to get the coal out of the ground as quickly as possible. There were not enough local workers and hundreds of thousands of people flocked to South Wales during the nineteenth century. The population of the Rhondda Valley alone rose from 850 in 1801 to 140 000 by 1921. The valleys of the coalfield began to fill up with mines, ironworks, canals, roads, railways, chapels and row upon row of terraced houses. Living conditions were often poor, with up to fifteen people crammed into a single terraced house. Employment in the coal mines rose to a peak of 230 000 by 1913 in 630 mines.

Blackband iron ore was found within the coal seams and there were large reserves of coking coal and limestone. These minerals provided the raw materials for the development of the iron and steel industry. A string of iron making towns grew up along the north eastern rim of the coalfield. The most important were Merthyr Tydfil and Ebbw Vale. Iron and steel from South Wales was sold all over the world.

The coal and steel industries attracted other industries into the region including tinplating, coke ovens, chemicals, copper, lead and zinc smelting. South Wales became one of Britain's most important industrial areas.

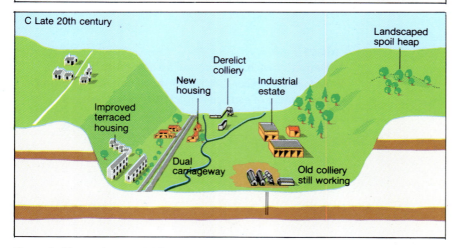

Figure A Change in a model South Wales valley

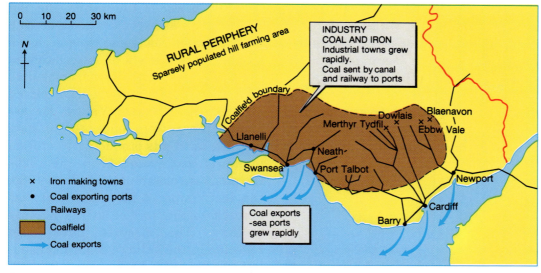

Figure B South Wales in the nineteenth century – industrial growth

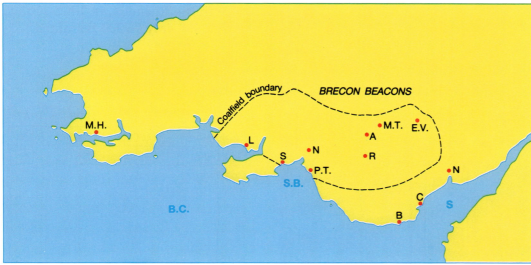

Figure C Outline map of South Wales

The bubble bursts

After a century of growth, South Wales faced disaster in the 1920s. Demand for coal and steel dropped rapidly. Coal output fell from 55 million tonnes in 1913 to 30 million tonnes by 1935. In 1923 there were 213 000 miners; by 1937 only 108 000 were left. In some valleys over 60 per cent of the men were out of work. The flood of people into South Wales was halted and reversed. Between 1921 and 1936 over 300 000 people left the region seeking work elsewhere, mainly in South-East England and the Midlands. South Wales entered a period of decline from which it has yet to emerge fully.

QUESTIONS

1 What was South Wales like before 1800?

2 'South Wales became one of Britain's most important industrial areas.' List the reasons which explain why this happened.

3 Copy the outline map of South Wales and, using your atlas to help you, complete the names of the towns, the sea areas and the rivers.

4 Using Figure A to help you, describe how a typical valley in the coalfield was altered by the growth of industry.

5 Study the table below:

Changes in the Welsh coal industry

Year	Coal production (million tonnes)	Coalminers (thousands)	Collieries
1913	55	230	630
1937	26	108	305

a) Calculate the percentage decline in coal production and the number of coalminers and collieries.

b) Explain the changes shown by the table.

6.2 South Wales 2

The table (Figure B) shows the extent of the decline in South Wales' traditional industries of coal and steel. The multiplier effect which accompanied the growth of the South Wales industrial region has operated in reverse in the valleys of the coalfield. Over a hundred pits have closed since 1960. The closure of each pit has resulted in a drop in the spending power of the people, the closure of shops and services and a decline in population as some people leave seeking work elsewhere. Associated industries such as coke ovens, smokeless fuel and chemical plants have closed also. In the Rhondda Valley, for example, there were once 40 000 men working in 54 pits producing 10 million tonnes of coal a year. Since the 1920s the pits have closed until, in June 1986, the last tonne of Rhondda coal was brought to the surface at the Maerdy Colliery. The closures have been reflected in the valley's declining population. In 1911 there were 168 000 people in the Rhondda, in 1961 100 300 and by 1986 only 75 000 remained.

Figure B Decline in South Wales' coal and steel industries

Indicators	1960	1970	1987
Coalminers	71 000	43 000	9 000
Coal mines	118	54	14
Coal output (million tonnes)	23	12	6
Iron & steel workers	61 000	55 000	12 000
Iron & steel works	11	7	2

The eastern and central coalfield Valleys face continued unemployment and decline. Unemployment figures of over 50 per cent are found in several coalfield communities. Some new industries have been attracted such as Hoover's washing machine factory at Merthyr Tydfil and Hitachi's television factory at Hirwaun. However, the Valleys hold

Figure A Two views of Trehafod in the Rhondda Valley, in 1927 and in 1988. Lewis Merthyr Colliery stands derelict in 1988, but in 1927 its smoke blackened the skies. Notice the disappearance of the other colliery, the railways and several terraces of houses. What else has changed?

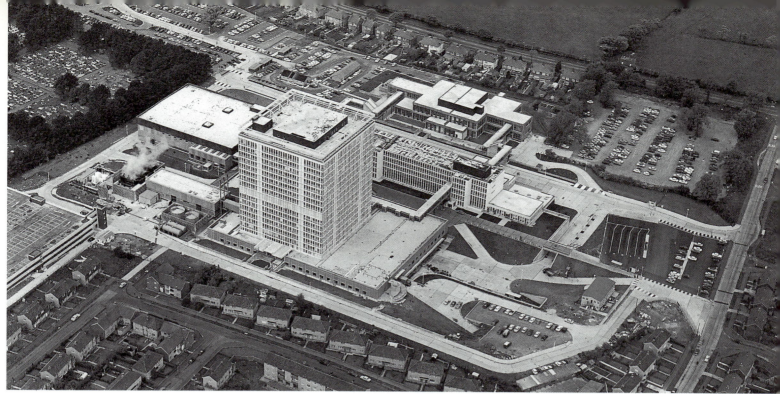

Figure C The Driver Vehicle Licensing Centre at Swansea

few attractions for large modern industry:
- There are few flat sites for large factories.
- The Valleys are inaccessible. The M4 motorway passes well to the south.
- Much of the housing is of poor quality.
- There is still much derelict land.

The industrial focus of South Wales has moved from the coalfield valleys to the coastal lowlands. Here are the large flat sites needed by modern industry and the transport links provided by the M4 motorway, the Inter-City railway to London, Cardiff Airport and the seaports of Swansea, Cardiff and Newport. The lowlands form the western extension of the Western Corridor, the high growth industrial region which stretches from London along the M4.

There are now over 14 000 jobs in high-tech industry in South Wales. Newport and Cardiff have attracted much of this development. At Cardiff televisions, telecommunications equipment, radiochemical isotopes and electronic games machines are among the high-tech products. The vehicle components industry has also been attracted to the coastal lowlands. Bridgend has a Ford engine plant, Swansea a Ford axles and transmissions factory and Llanelli an Austin Rover radiators works. Several important government offices have been built in the region including the Driver Vehicle Licensing Centre and the Land Registry at Swansea, the Royal Mint at Llantrisant and the Inland Revenue and Ministry of Defence at Cardiff.

QUESTIONS

1. Refer to the table opposite and answer the following questions:
   a) How many jobs were lost in the coal and steel industries between 1960 and 1987?
   b) What is the percentage decline in (i) the number of coal mines and (ii) coal output?
   c) How do you explain the large difference in these percentages?

2. Why has little new industry developed in the coalfield Valleys?

3. a) Explain why the industrial focus of South Wales has moved from the Valleys to the coastal lowlands.
   b) What types of employment have been attracted to the coastal lowlands?

4. You have lived in the Rhondda Valley all your life. You worked at the Maerdy Colliery until it closed in 1986 when you took early retirement. Write about the changes you have seen over the last fifty years in the Rhondda. What were your feelings when you left the colliery for the last time? How has the disappearance of the coal industry affected life in the Rhondda? Do you think that the government should have kept some of the collieries open? What are your hopes and fears for the future?

6.3 The port industries of Rotterdam

Ports are very important locations for industry. This is because they are *transhipment* points where goods are unloaded from one form of transport and loaded onto another. Since this unloading has to take place anyway, a factory at a port gains the advantage of using both sea and land transport with only one loading cost. A port location allows bulky materials to be used since ships can handle the bulkiest cargoes easily. Many port industries are based on the import of bulk raw materials.

Figure A shows part of the Port of Rotterdam in the Netherlands. This is one of the most important single concentrations of industry in Europe. The industrial sites cover vast areas of flat land, much of it reclaimed from the sea. The industries make use of the facilities of Rotterdam, the largest seaport in the world. Rotterdam became a major port after the construction of the New Waterway in 1872. This 40 kilometre long artificial waterway links the centre of Rotterdam with the North Sea. The New Waterway is lined with berths and industries. The first were built in central Rotterdam, but as ships were built larger and larger and the port's trade increased, larger berths were built towards the sea. Vessels of over 350 000 tonnes can enter the Maasvlakte terminal. Industries using bulk cargoes such as oil, mineral ores and grain, became concentrated around the deepwater berths close to the sea. Industries processing imported raw materials developed further inland along the New Waterway.

Figure A Europoort and Maasvlakte Docks at Rotterdam – the world's busiest seaport

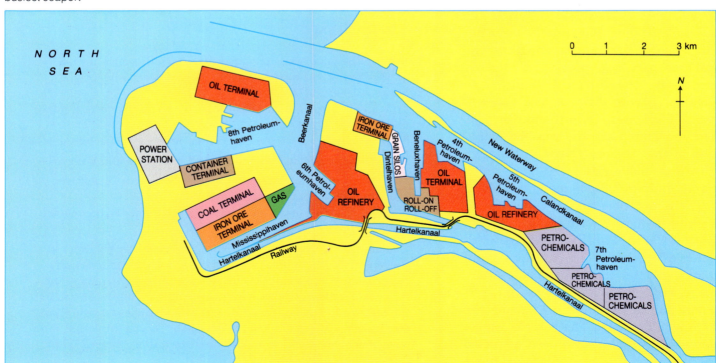

Figure B Europoort and Maasvlakte

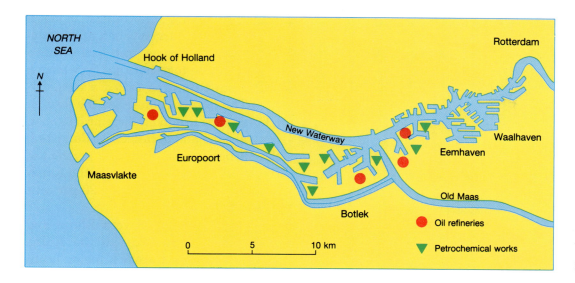

Figure C The port of Rotterdam

Figure C shows the major industrial sites. The main industries are:

- Oil refining: five large refineries have a combined capacity of 90 million tonnes. This makes Rotterdam Europe's leading oil refining centre.
- Oil storage: several oil terminals store crude oil awaiting shipment to smaller ports in northern Europe.
- Petrochemicals: there are ten large processing plants.
- Coal and iron ore are stored in terminals while they await shipment to smaller ports.
- Shipbuilding: the Verolme shipbuilding and ship repair yard is the main survivor of a once thriving industry at Rotterdam. Construction of offshore drilling equipment has become important.
- Engineering: Rotterdam has many engineering and electronic companies.
- Vegetable oil processing: several plants process oils and fats into foodstuffs, soap and washing powders.
- Food processing: grain milling, tobacco, sugar refining, brewing, chocolate, coffee, biscuits and cakes.

This great concentration of industry has resulted in problems of air and water pollution in Rotterdam. It was partly because of objections to the increased pollution that plans for a steelworks at Maasvlakte were scrapped during the 1970s.

QUESTIONS

1. Why is a port a suitable location for industry?
2. Using your atlas to help you, describe the site of Rotterdam.
3. List six industries in Rotterdam.
4. Why has Rotterdam become 'one of the most important single concentrations of industry in Europe'?
5. Study the table below:

Port of Rotterdam trade in 1983

Commodity	Tonnage (million tonnes)
Crude oil	75
Oil products	35
Iron ore	30
Animal feed	11
Chemicals	11
Coal	11
Vegetable oils and fats	7
Grain	6
Minerals	3
Other bulk cargoes	3
General cargo	40
Total	**232**

   a) Draw a pie graph to illustrate these statistics.
   b) What was the total tonnage of bulk cargo handled by the Port of Rotterdam in 1983?
   c) What percentage of the total cargo was bulk cargo?
6. Study Figures A and B.
   a) In which direction was the camera pointing in Figure A?
   b) Name the waterways at A and B.
   c) Name the dock areas C and D.
   d) Name the industrial sites at E and F.
7. What do you think are the advantages and disadvantages to Rotterdam of the large scale industry in the area?

6.4 The Randstad

Figure A The Randstad
Figure B Offices in central Rotterdam

As Figure A shows, Rotterdam is just a part of a much larger urban and industrial region. Towns and cities have grown so close together that they form a single built up area called a *conurbation*. The conurbation takes the form of a horse-shoe around a more or less open central zone and is called the Randstad. Six million people, that is 42 per cent of the Dutch population, live in the Randstad although it covers only 20 per cent of the country.

The delta of the Rivers Rhine and Maas are the gateway to the Rhine Valley which is Europe's major economic axis. In the past this made the Western Netherlands a major centre of trade and commerce, but industry was limited by the lack of raw materials and fuels. Until the twentieth century, Dutch industry consisted of port industries such as sugar refining, grain milling and tobacco manufacture. Developments in engineering and chemicals occurred in the early years of this century, but it is since 1945 that the most rapid expansion of Dutch industry has happened.

Manufacturing industry

Dutch industry is concentrated in the Randstad where there are many locational advantages:

● Access to major seaports (Rotterdam and Amsterdam) and Amsterdam International Airport (Schiphol).

● Excellent communications by road, rail and inland waterway.

● A concentrated, rich urban population providing both a market and a skilled workforce.

● Access to the capital city (Amsterdam) and the seat of government (The Hague), important for finance and administration.

Manufacturing employs 250 000 people in the Randstad (31 per cent of the Dutch total). Unlike Paris or London, the urban functions of the Randstad are not concentrated in one vast city but are spread in different parts of the conurbation.

Service industry

Manufacturing industry has declined in importance in the Netherlands, just as it has in other West European countries. In 1960 42 per cent of the Dutch workforce were employed in manufacturing, by 1986 the figure was only 27 per cent. There has been a rapid increase in service industry: 47 per cent of the total workforce in 1960, 67 per cent by 1986.

Fifteen per cent of the Dutch workforce is employed in government offices, over half of them in The Hague. The Hague is also the headquarters of many large companies including Shell and Esso. In order to meet the growing need for office space new offices have been built in outlying suburbs, and a number of government departments have been moved to other regions of the Netherlands in order to relieve congestion in the Randstad and to provide jobs in areas of higher unemployment such as the North-East and South Limburg. In 1986 this policy was stopped. It was decided that no more transfers of government departments would take place because of the rising level of unemployment in the Randstad itself.

Amsterdam is the Dutch capital and the centre of finance, insurance and banking. Amsterdam also houses the headquarters of many international companies including Heineken (beer) and Fokker (aircraft). In addition to office employment, retailing is very important, Amsterdam being the major shopping centre. Offices and shops have formed important parts of redevelopment schemes in the cities of the Randstad. In Utrecht, for example, the Hoog-Catharijne project is a large complex of shops, offices, a concert hall and conference centre. An area of nineteenth century housing was demolished to make way for the development, which has been built on either side of Utrecht's central railway station. Over 8000 jobs have been created in this centre.

Figure C The Fokker 100 twin-jet airliner – made in the Randstad

QUESTIONS

1 a) What is the Randstad?
b) Where is it?

2 Study Figure A.
a) Draw up a table using the headings shown below:
City, Population, Main Functions.
b) List the cities of the Randstad in order of their population size and add their main functions.
c) Draw a sketch map of the Western Netherlands showing the location of these cities.
d) Draw a divided bar 14.5 cm long to represent the total population of the Netherlands (14.5 million). Shade in the correct amount representing the total population of the Randstad and give your bar a suitable title.

3 Link these famous Dutch companies with their products:
Company: Philips Shell Heineken Unilever Hoogovens Fokker
Products: steel beer aircraft electronics oil and chemicals food

3 a) Explain the term 'conurbation'.
b) How does the Randstad conurbation differ from other conurbations?

4 Study the table below:

Concentration of certain factors in the Randstad

Factor	Percentage of Dutch total
Area	20
Population	42
Manufacturing workforce	31
Tertiary industry workforce	48

a) Draw four simple pie charts to show this information.
b) Explain why Dutch industry is concentrated in the Randstad.

6.5 The Western Corridor

Swindon

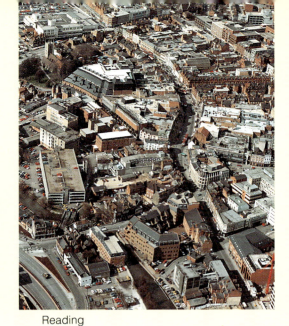
Reading

Figure A The Western Corridor

SWINDON
Pop: 160 000
Rapidly growing high-tech industries including Intel, Logica and Plessey micro-electronics. Major office centre including Allied Dunbar and Nationwide insurance, Burmah oil.

READING
Pop: 135 300
Rapidly growing high-tech industries include Digital, Hewlett Packard, Motorola and ICL computers, Panasonic, Hitachi and Norsk Data micro-electronics.

SLOUGH
Pop: 98 600
Slough Trading Estate dates from the 1920s. Food and metal industries. In the Green Belt with little room for new development so little high-tech industry.

BRISTOL
Pop: 394 000
Rapid growth in high-tech industry. Firms include Hewlett Packard, Digital Research, IBM and ICL computers, British Aerospace, Rolls Royce aero-engines, Marconi avionics. Many major offices including Commercial Union, Guardian Royal Exchange and Phoenix insurance.

NEWBURY
Pop: 30 600
Many new firms including Bayer chemicals and Sony electronics distribution centre.

BRACKNELL
Pop: 90 700
Rapidly growing New Town. Many high-tech companies including Ferranti, 3M, ICI, Racal, Honeywell and British Aerospace micro-electronics and computers.

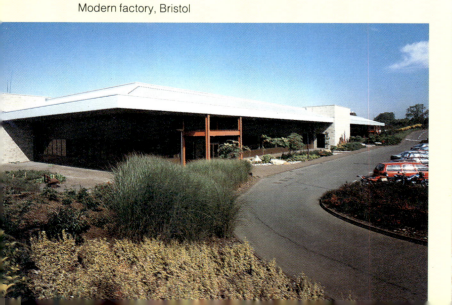
Modern factory, Bristol

Bracknell

Figure A shows Britain's new industrial axis, the Western Corridor. It spreads westwards along the M4 motorway from Heathrow Airport to Bristol and beyond into South Wales. At or near each junction on the M4 you will find business parks, industrial estates, warehouses and office complexes.

Much of the growth in employment along the Western Corridor has occurred at the expense of London. In comparison with London the Corridor offers:

- lower land costs
- lower rates
- a more attractive environment
- less congested roads and services
- lower house prices
- greenfield industrial sites

Much of the new employment in the Western Corridor is in high-technology industry and offices (Figure A). Figure B shows the impressive population growth figures of the districts along the Corridor.

Reading

Reading, with a population of 130 000, is the centre of a rapidly growing urban area of over a quarter of a million people. Reading's location is the key to its success. The M4 motorway passes to the south of the town, linking Reading to central London (55 km) and Heathrow Airport (32 km). Reading's long established industries of biscuits, brewing and food processing have declined. High-technology firms have moved into Reading, providing much new employment. Computer manufacturers such as Digital Equipment, precision engineering companies such as Hitachi and office employers such as Prudential Assurance have chosen Reading.

Many of the new jobs are for highly skilled people and the semi- and unskilled workers in Reading have been left out in the cold. Unemployment rates in some of the large council estates reach over 20 per cent. However, Reading's main problems are concerned with how to cope with rapid growth. Housing is in great demand so prices have risen quickly. Improvements in Reading's road system have not kept pace with the increase in traffic. Nearly half a million people travel into central Reading to work every day. Traffic congestion has been given as a reason for the failure of some Reading companies to expand their factories; instead they have built new factories in other towns further along the Western Corridor.

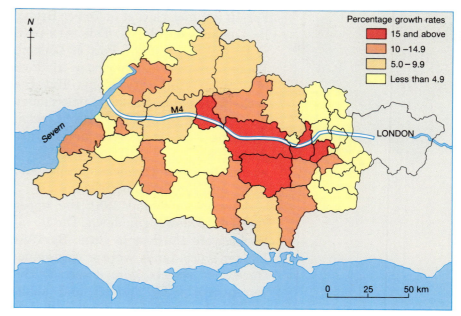

Figure B Population growth rates in districts in and around the Western Corridor

QUESTIONS

1. a) What is the Western Corridor?
   b) What is the distance from the edge of Greater London to
   (i) Newbury (ii) Swindon (iii) Bristol?

2. Design a poster intended to attract companies to Newbury. Your poster should emphasise the advantages which Newbury offers in comparison to London.

3. Study Figure B. Does the map support the view that the Western Corridor is one of Britain's fastest growing areas?

4. 'Reading's location is the key to its success.' Why is this?

5. a) How has the employment structure of Reading changed in recent years?
   b) Despite Reading's rapid growth in employment, some areas of the town have unemployment rates of over 20 per cent. Explain this apparent contradiction.

6. a) What problems have been created by Reading's rapid growth?
   b) How might these problems be solved?

6.6 Why not move to the centre of London?

For 12 kilometres east of Tower Bridge lie London's docklands. This area used to be the heart of the Port of London. There were over 30 000 jobs in the Port of London Authority alone. But the docks were old and small. Little money was spent on them. The Port of London Authority decided to invest in its larger docks down river at Tilbury in Essex where the River Thames is deeper and wider and can take larger ships.

Between 1967 and 1981 the upper docks were slowly run down. The Royal Docks were the last to close. By 1981 London's docklands were a wasteland. Once-busy streets were deserted. The warehouses were derelict and abandoned, the cranes rusting and dismantled. Vandalism was common. Everywhere were signs of neglect and decline. Wealthier people had moved away, leaving the poor in despair. Unemployment rates topped 30 per cent. Nine out of ten of the people in the docklands lived in flats and houses owned by the local councils. The population of the docklands fell from 71 000 in 1971 to only 39 000 by 1981.

The London Docklands Development Corporation

The docklands showed all the signs of inner city decay. Yet the closure of the docks presented a great opportunity for revitalizing the area. Attempts were made during the 1970s to start this, but not enough money was made available. In 1981 the government set up the London Docklands Development Corporation (LDDC) to take over new developments in the area from the local councils. The LDDC had full control over planning and running the new growth in the docklands. It also had plenty of money available for land purchase, construction of services and grants to new companies wishing to move into the area.

The LDDC were helped by the setting up of an Enterprise Zone in the Isle of Dogs in 1982. Companies establishing themselves here have a 10 year period free from rates, do not have to pay land development tax and face fewer planning restrictions.

Employment

The old port industries have gone. New factories and offices have been encouraged to set up in the docklands. Over 400 new companies have moved in and 10 000 new jobs have been created. Most of the new factories are small units engaged in electronics and telecommunications. Several national newspapers have opened new printing

Figure A Three views of the changing scene in the Royal Docks – (left to right) 1946, 1986 and 1988

works. A number of superstores have been built. There is a plan for a vast office development at Canary Wharf in the Isle of Dogs. Three office blocks will be built rising to over 260 metres, making them the tallest buildings in Europe. It is hoped that over 45 000 jobs will be provided, mainly in financial services.

Housing

Over 25 000 new houses have been built. The LDDC has insisted that some cheaper houses and flats should be provided, but many of them have been resold at a high profit by their first owners. Many of the new homes are expensive, over £400 000 in some cases.

Transport

One of the major problems facing the redevelopment of the docklands was its poor transport links. Several transport improvements have been made:

1 £500 million has been spent on new and improved roads. A link road to the M11 motorway has been built. A new suspension bridge, the East London River Crossing, is planned.

2 The Docklands Light Railway linking the Isle of Dogs with Tower Hill in Central London was opened in 1987. There are 16 stations along the 12 km route. It is planned to extend the light railway into the Royal Docks.

3 London City Airport was opened in 1987 on the long quay separating the Royal Albert and King George V dock. The short runway is used by Short Take-Off and Landing (STOL) airliners flying services to major UK and West European cities. Over one million passengers a year use the airport.

4 A high speed river bus operates on the Thames. Services have been proposed from as far west as Chelsea and as far east as Southend-on-Sea.

The LDDC has been heavily criticized by local councils and many local people in the docklands. They claim that the LDDC is too concerned with attracting middle and upper class people into this traditionally working class area. The new high technology industries and offices provide few jobs for the local people. The council homes in which over half of docklands' population still live, remain neglected and decaying.

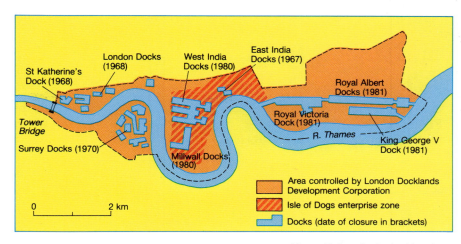

Figure B London's docklands

Figure C The Docklands Light Railway

QUESTIONS

1 Where are the London docklands?
2 Why did the docklands become 'a wasteland'?
3 a) What is the LDDC?
   b) When was the LDDC established?
   c) What was the LDDC's aim?
4 Why are new companies especially attracted to the Isle of Dogs?
5 What new employment has been established in the docklands?
6 How has the accessibility of the docklands been improved?
7 How have the policies of the LDDC been criticized?
8 One of the most controversial developments in the docklands has been the London City Airport. Why do you think the airport was strongly opposed by many local people?
9 Design an advertising poster for the LDDC designed to attract new companies into the docklands.

Unit 6 ASSESSMENT

1. a) Name the six towns and the airport shown on Figure A. (7 marks)
   b) Name the motorway and the bridge. (2 marks)

Figure A

2. Study the advertisement for Newport (Figure B).
   a) Where is Newport? (1 mark)
   b) Which 'corridor' is referred to in the advertisement? (1 mark)
   c) List five advantages of the corridor. (5 marks)
   d) What special advantages does the advertisement claim for Newport? (4 marks)
   e) What type of industry is especially attracted to the towns along the corridor? (2 marks)
   f) Why would a company wish to leave London for a new location along the corridor? (5 marks)

Figure B

3 Study the table below:
   a) Draw a line graph to illustrate the statistics in the table. (7 marks)
   b) i) Which town has suffered the highest population loss between 1961 and 1985? (1 mark)
      ii) Explain the reasons for the rapid population decline in that town. (5 marks)
   c) i) Which is the only town to have increased in population between 1961 and 1985? (1 mark)
      ii) Explain why this town has not suffered the rapid population decline of the others in the table. (3 marks)

Population change in selected South Wales towns

Town	Population (thousands)			
	1961	1971	1981	1985
Newport	129	137	134	130
Pontypridd	37	35	33	32
Rhondda	100	89	82	79
Merthyr Tydfil	67	63	61	59
Cardiff	290	288	274	279

4 Study the table below:
   a) Which is the least important method of transport used? (1 mark)
   b) Which country is linked by pipeline to Rotterdam? (1 mark)
   c) i) What percentage of the traffic to West Germany is carried by barge? (1 mark)
      ii) Explain why barge transport is so important in Rotterdam's trade with West Germany. (2 marks)
      iii) What are the advantages and disadvantages of barges as a means of transport? (4 marks)
   d) i) Name three major industries in Rotterdam. (3 marks)
      ii) Explain why these industries have developed at Rotterdam. (6 marks)

Goods carried from Rotterdam to parts of its hinterland

Method of transport	Hinterland (million tonnes per year)			
	West Germany	Belgium	France	Switzerland
By ship	2.2	0.1	0.9	0
By barge	32.8	3.5	1.8	1.4
By rail	0.3	0	0.1	0.1
By road	1.0	0.4	0.2	0.1
By pipeline	14.7	0	0	0
Total	51.0	4.0	3.0	1.6

5 a) What problems faced the London docklands in 1981? (4 marks)
  b) Describe the measures taken to develop the docklands since 1981. (9 marks)

TOTAL: 75 marks

Details for pupil profile sheet Unit 6

Knowledge and understanding

1 Blackband iron ore
2 Industrial decline
3 Transhipment point
4 Port industry
5 Conurbation
6 Randstad
7 London Docklands Development Corporation

Skills

1 Interpret change over time from diagrams
2 Calculate percentages
3 Role play
4 Draw a pie graph
5 Interpret an aerial photograph
6 interpret a map of population change
7 Drawing a bar graph
8 Presenting textual information in the form of a table
9 Interpreting a newspaper advertisement
10 Designing a newspaper advertisement

Values

1 The social effects of industrial decline
2 The impersonal nature of large scale planning

Unit 7: Third World industry

7.1 The importance of industry

Figure A The domination of export trade by a single resource in certain developing countries

Country	Major export	Percentage of total exports
Saudi Arabia	Oil	99
Nigeria	Oil	92
Zambia	Copper	92
Mauritania	Iron ore	91
Gambia	Peanuts	84
Sudan	Cotton	66
Chad	Cotton	60
Chile	Copper	59
Burma	Rice	50

Figure B Manufactured goods as a percentage of total exports in selected countries

Country	1974	1984
Argentina	19.5	20.4
Brazil	18.1	31.6
India	52.9	54.7
South Korea	82.9	88.5
Indonesia	4.3	8.1
Kenya	7.7	10.7
Ghana	11.2	15.1
Jamaica	4.9	10.0

Most people in the developing world work in agriculture. The economies of most developing countries depend upon the export of primary products: cash crops, minerals and forest products (Figure A). However, many developing countries have tried to increase the role of manufacturing industry in recent years as Figure B shows.

Manufacturing industry has often been seen as the answer to the poverty of the developing world. Manufacturing has several potential advantages:

- It offers higher wages than farming.
- It can make use of the raw materials found in many developing countries. Exports of manufactured goods earn much more than exports of raw materials.
- It reduces the need for expensive imports of manufactured goods.
- It demands a skilled, educated workforce and a technological infrastructure of roads, telephones, electricity and so on.

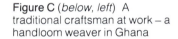

Figure C (below, left) A traditional craftsman at work – a handloom weaver in Ghana

Figure D (below, right) The Embraer aircraft factory at Sao Jose dos Campos, Brazil

Multi-national companies

Several developing countries are now among the world's leading industrial nations such as India, Brazil and South Korea. These nations are keen to follow the example of Japan which has become a developed country through building a powerful manufacturing sector. Few developing countries can afford to set up their own manufacturing industries without outside help. In some cases aid from foreign governments may be used. Often multi-national companies are invited to set up new factories. Multi-national companies are very large firms based in developed countries. They are attracted by the low wages of workers in developing countries and the lack of strikes. Multi-national companies can usually negotiate good deals with the governments of developing countries, saving money on tax, rates and rents.

The jobs and money provided by multi-national companies are welcome to developing countries. Less welcome is the influence that some multi-nationals have had on the internal affairs of some developing countries. It has been claimed that multi-nationals have helped to rig elections, change government policies and even overthrow governments. The multi-nationals have more money and power than many governments and can pull out of those countries whose policies they do not approve of. The largest multi-national is the Exxon Corporation of the USA, which includes Esso. Only three developing countries, China, India and Brazil, have a higher annual income than Exxon.

It should not be forgotten that there are many traditional craft industries which are important in developing countries: handloom weaving, wood carving, basket weaving, pottery and iron making are major examples. Some of these are threatened by the growth of mechanized industry.

Lonrho's interests in Africa

- **Gold** mines in Ghana and Zimbabwe
- **Coffee** estates in Zimbabwe and Ghana
- **Tea** estates in Malawi, Kenya and Tanzania
- **Farm machinery** in Zambia
- **Paint** manufacture in Zambia
- **Textiles** in Zimbabwe and Malawi
- **Truck** and **bus** manufacture in Zimbabwe

Lonrho is a UK-based multi-national company

Figure E

QUESTIONS

1. What do you understand by the term 'primary product'?
2. a) Draw divided bars, 100 mm long, to represent the export trade of each of the nine countries in Figure A.
   b) Shade in the section of the bar proportional to the percentage of total exports of the major export commodity. Write the name of the commodity on the bar.
3. a) Copy out the table in Figure B and add a third column showing by how many per cent the percentage contribution of manufactured goods to total exports increased between 1974 and 1984.
   b) Which three countries showed the highest increase?
4. a) What do you understand by the term 'multi-national company'?
   b) Name four examples.
5. Why do you think that large multi-national companies have so much power and influence in some developing countries?
6. Study Figure E.
   a) On an outline map of Africa shade in the countries where Lonrho has interests.
   b) Make two lists of the advantages and disadvantages which multi-national companies may bring to developing countries.
   c) In your view which of your lists is most important?

7.2 Heavy industry in India

Heavy industries process raw materials into basic products such as iron, steel and chemicals which can then be used by many other manufacturing industries. Concentrations of heavy industry in the developing world are rare. One of the most important is the Damodar Basin in North-East India.

The River Damodar is a tributary of the River Hooghly on which the city of Calcutta stands. There are many reasons which help to explain why this region has become one of Asia's leading centres of heavy industry:

• The Damodar Basin has a range of natural resources including coal, iron ore and bauxite (Figure A). The Indian government decided in the 1950s to develop basic heavy industries which could make use of these mineral resources.

• The region contains India's largest coalfields, inluding most of the country's coking coal. Iron ore and limestone are available nearby. These resources have provided a base for the iron and steel industry.

• Heavy industry needs large amounts of electricity. Hydro-electric power stations have been built where the River Damodar has been dammed. The largest is the Durgapur barrage. Several coal-fuelled power stations have also been built.

• There is a ready market for the region's steel within easy reach. Most of it is taken by rail and road to the shipyards, car plant and heavy engineering factories of Calcutta.

Integrated steelworks cost a great deal of money to build. India was a poor country in the 1950s and it had to rely on aid from other countries to develop the steel industry. The Jamshedpur works was built by the British when India was a British colony. The Durgapur works was built with British help after India became independent. The complete steelworks was built by British engineers using equipment built in Britain. More recent steelworks have been built in partnership with other countries and many of the parts have been made in India. West Germany helped with the Rourkela plant and the USSR helped with Bokara. By the 1970s the Indians were designing and building new steelworks with little outside help.

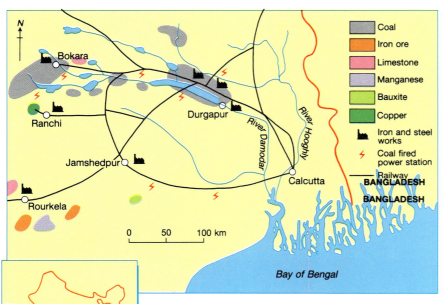

Figure A The Damodar Valley industrial area, India

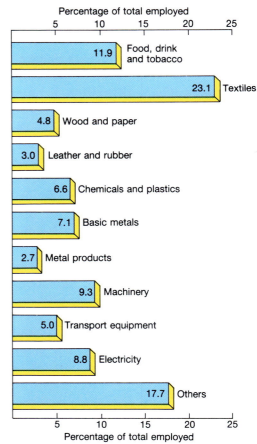

Figure B Employment in Indian manufacturing industry

Figure C Bokaro Steelworks – inside and out

Annual Indian steel production is about 10 million tonnes. It provides the basis for a range of new industries. There are also chemical, cement, aluminium smelting, textile, electrical and heavy engineering factories. The Damodar Basin–Calcutta axis employs 30 per cent of India's total industrial workforce. India's steelworks employ much larger workforces than the steelworks of developed countries. For example, the Durgapur works employs 28 000 people to produce under a million tonnes of steel a year; the Port Talbot works in South Wales employs 4 750 people to produce 3 million tonnes. This makes Indian steel very expensive, despite the low wage rates of Indian workers, but the Government has decided that employment is more important than profit.

On one level the development of heavy industry in the Damodar Basin has been a success. It has attracted other industries and is India's most important industrial area. However, the developments have affected only a small part of India's population of 750 million, 40 per cent of whom live in dire poverty. Only about 25 million people work in modern industry and there are another 18 million seeking such jobs. As a result the Indian Government turned its attention in the 1970s to smaller scale industrial development throughout the country aimed at benefiting more people. By the late 1980s a balanced programme of industrial development was under way, aimed at increasing industrial capacity and efficiency and increasing industrial employment, especially in less favoured areas. This has caused attention to be redirected at heavier industry, in particular at the manufacture of motor vehicles.

QUESTIONS

1 Where is the Damodar Basin?
2 List six natural resources located in the Damodar Basin.
3 a) Why is there a high demand for electricity in the Damodar Basin?
   b) How is this high demand met?
4 Describe the steel industry which has developed in the Damodar Basin.
5 Study the table below:

Comparative coal statistics in 1985

Country	Coal production (million tonnes)	Collieries	Coal miners	Output per manshift (tonnes)
India	147	400	710 000	0.8
UK	95	109	120 000	3.5

   a) What is the average production per colliery in (i) India and (ii) the UK?
   b) What does this suggest about the size of Indian collieries?
   c) Why does the Indian coal industry continue to employ such a large workforce?
6 Why did the Indian government turn its attention to smaller scale industrial developments in the 1970s?

7.3 Brazilian motor industry

Figure A Leading motor car producers in 1990

Country	Car production (millions)
1. Japan	9.9
2. USA	6.3
3. West Germany	4.7
4. France	3.3
5. Italy	2.3
6. Spain	1.7
7. UK	1.3
8. USSR	1.2
9. Canada	1.1
10. South Korea	0.9
11. Brazil	0.8
12. Australia	0.4

Figure B (*top*) Aerial view of the Ford car factory at Sao Paulo

Figure C (*bottom*) Inside the Ford assembly plant

Look at Figure A. All the countries in the table are among the world's leading industrial nations, except one – Brazil. Brazil is a developing country yet it has one of the world's major motor industries. Why?

Until the 1950s Brazil had no motor industry. The few cars on Brazil's roads were imported. The market for cars was small and concentrated in the rich cities of the south-east, especially Rio de Janeiro and São Paulo. In 1956 the government of Brazil decided to develop a motor industry. This was hoped to bring thousands of jobs in modern industry and help to raise the living standards of Brazilians. It was also hoped to encourage the growth of companies making parts. Many new industrial skills would be learned by Brazilian workers and management which would help other areas of Brazil's economy.

Brazil was a poor country and had no experience of making motor vehicles or the machines and factories which build them. Brazil would have to depend upon help from the rich industrial countries. But why should these countries help Brazil?

The government decided to put high taxes on cars imported into Brazil. It offered loans, grants and cheap land to foreign car firms willing to build factories in Brazil. The import taxes meant that Brazil's small, but growing, demand for cars would be largely supplied by the new factories. This made good business sense to the giant car companies of the USA, Europe and Japan:

- They could build and operate modern factories at a cheap price.
- They would have a guaranteed market within Brazil and could supply the demands of other South American countries.
- The low wage rates of Brazilian workers were attractive.
- The strong military government of Brazil meant that there would be little problem of strike action by the workers.

Several foreign multi-national companies built car works in Brazil. Volkswagen of West Germany and Ford and General Motors of the USA opened factories at São Paulo. The Italian company, Fiat, opened a plant at Belo Horizonte. The motor industry now employs 160 000 people, nearly 10 per cent of Brazil's industrial workforce. The foreign companies have been able to cash in on the rapidly growing demand for cars in Brazil. They have been able to produce cars more cheaply than in Europe and the USA and have been able to export cars from Brazil all over the world including to Europe and the USA themselves. Vehicle exports now make up five per cent of Brazil's export earnings.

Of course there have been some problems in the development of the Brazilian motor industry:

• Part of the profits are taken out of Brazil by the foreign companies.

• The growing number of motor cars has greatly increased Brazil's oil imports bill.

• The chance of factory work has encouraged millions of people to move into Sao Paulo and Belo Horizonte from the poverty-stricken rural areas of Brazil.

• The wages paid to the workers on the assembly lines are too low to support a family. The foreign companies have received much bad publicity from people accusing them of exploiting the workers.

Figure D (*above left*) The Central Business District of Sao Paulo

Figure E (*above*) Many Brazilian workers have to live in *favelas* like these

QUESTIONS

1 a) Draw a bar graph to show the twelve leading car producers in 1990.
   b) Why is it unusual to find Brazil included in such a list?

2 a) When did the Brazilian government decide to develop a motor industry?
   b) What were the aims of such developments?

3 What were the advantages to a multi-national company of building a car factory in Brazil?

4 Using an outline map of Brazil and your atlas to help you:
   a) Mark the locations of the four large Brazilian car plants.
   b) Label the following major cities: Sao Paulo, Rio de Janeiro, Belo Horizonte, Brasilia, Salvador, Recife, Porto Alegre, Fortaleza, Curitiba.
   c) Shade in the areas with a population density of over 50 persons per square kilometre.
   d) Where do you think the main demand for cars is in Brazil?

5 How successful has the growth of the Brazilian motor industry been?

7.4 The newly industrialized countries

An increasing number of developing countries have put their faith in building up manufacturing industries. They are trying to follow the example set by Japan in the 1950s and Brazil in the 1970s. Figure B shows the major newly industrialized countries (NICs).

The majority of the NICs are located around the shores of the Pacific Ocean. The 'Pacific Basin' has been hailed as 'the industrial region of the future'. It includes the developed countries of Australia, New Zealand, the west coast of the USA and the eastern coastal areas of the USSR and China. Most attention has been focussed on the NICs, especially South Korea, Taiwan, Hong Kong, Singapore, Indonesia and Mexico. These countries have rapid growth rates in manufacturing and exports.

The success of the NICs is based on exporting manufactured goods, especially to developed countries. Most NICs began by making textiles and clothes. Later light electronics and assembly industries were developed.

Figure A (*left*) Singapore's CBD – signs of high-rise prosperity

Figure B (*below*) NICs – the Pacific Basin

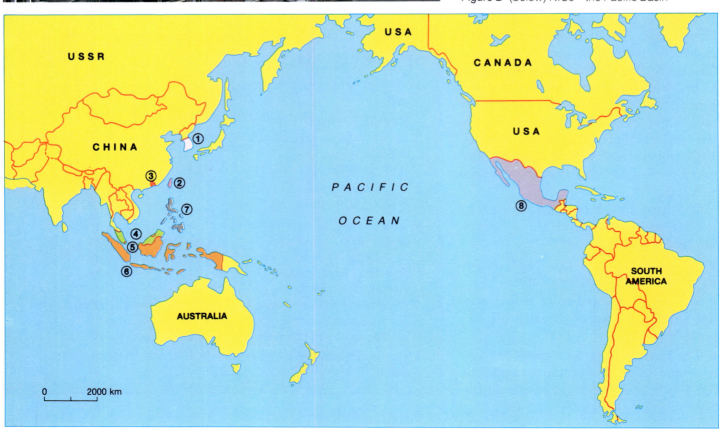

These industries have quite a high demand for labour and the NICs had the advantage of low wage rates compared with the developed countries. Companies from Europe, the USA and Japan rushed to build assembly plants in the NICs to supply the booming demands of people in the developed world and make as much profit as possible. Local businessmen set up companies also, some of which, such as Hyundai of South Korea, have grown into companies of worldwide importance. Many of the workers in the new industries have to work long hours in bad conditions for very low wages.

Once industry is established in the NICs their governments are keen to move on from low skill/low paid manufacturing because this mainly involves assembling components made elsewhere. The governments want to build new factories to make the components themselves. Another aim is to develop high-technology products such as computers, computer peripherals, video cameras and recorders which require more skilled and more highly paid labour.

As the wages increase the countries can no longer make things like clothes and radios cheaply; the multi-national companies close their factories and move elsewhere. The NICs have to begin to stand on their own, but they face tremendous problems in competing on world markets with the products of developed countries. Many NICs will have got into debt. Banks from the developed countries are very keen to lend money to the NICs to build new factories, roads, telephone systems etc. However, the loans often involve high rates of interest payments. For example, it has been calculated that Mexico needs to spend 35 per cent of its export earnings on paying the interest on its debts. The NICs have to keep growing rapidly if they are to repay the loans, and further growth needs more loans!

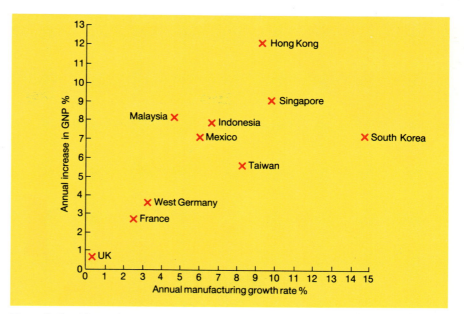

Figure C Rapid growth

QUESTIONS

1 What is a NIC?

2 a) Copy Figure B and name the NICs shown on the map.
   b) Where are most of the NICs located?

3 Study Figure C.
   a) What is the annual manufacturing growth rate of (i) South Korea (ii) Hong Kong (iii) Singapore (iv) Taiwan (v) Indonesia (vi) UK?
   b) Which two countries have the highest annual increase in GNP?

4 Study the table below:

Leading producers of radios and televisions in 1972 and 1982

Radios (millions)	1972	1982	Televisions (millions)	1972	1982
Hong Kong	1	42	Japan	14	13
Japan	25	14	USA	10	10
USSR	9	9	USSR	7	8
USA	16	8	South Korea	0	6
South Korea	3	6	Taiwan	1	5
West Germany	6	3	West Germany	3	4
Poland	1	2	Brazil	1	3
Indonesia	0.4	2	UK	3	2
Belgium	1	2	France	2	2
France	3	2	Italy	2	2
UK	2	0.4	Singapore	0	2
World total	81	142	World total	52	70

   a) Which three countries had the greatest increases in production?
   b) What advantages do these countries have for the assembly of radios and TVs?

5 a) Why do multi-nationals rush to build plants in the NICs?
   b) Why do multi-national companies often close these factories and move elsewhere after a few years?

7.5 Made in Korea

Korea was divided into two independent countries, the communist North Korea and the capitalist South Korea. Over a million people, mostly Korean civilians, were killed in the Korean War, which ended in 1953. Both countries were on their knees, battered and poverty-stricken.

Figure A South Korea

Figure B Seoul, capital of South Korea

Since the end of the war both countries have made impressive progress. North Korea has developed an advanced industrial economy based upon heavy industry (steel, oil refining and heavy engineering), on textiles and a growing agricultural sector. With a national income per person of over $1000, North Korea is one of the wealthier developing countries. South Korea's progress has been even more impressive.

South Korea

In 1960 South Korea was one of the world's poorest countries with a national income per person of less than $100. By 1986 this had risen to over $2000 per person making South Korea one of the richest and most successful of the newly industrializing countries. Shipbuilding and steel were the base for South Korea's industrial revolution.

Shipbuilding

The South Korean government invested $200 million in the shipbuilding industry during the late 1960s. Shipbuilding was seen as a suitable industry for the country's skilled and cheap labour force and as the best customer for the country's growing iron and steel industry. By 1982 South Korea was the world's second most important shipbuilding nation, launching 10 per cent of the world's ships. Hyundai owns the world's largest shipyard at Ulsan. It can build 40 vessels simultaneously, using the latest technology. South Korea has won orders in the face of competition from all other shipbuilding nations. Its shipbuilding industry has prospered while the industries of such countries as Britain and West Germany have collapsed.

Many new industries have been developed with an emphasis upon modern engineering and electronics. Televisions, radios, video recorders, computers, disc drives and machine tools are all appearing with the 'Made in Korea' label. The growth of the car industry has been rapid. Daewoo has an assembly plant at Pupyung developed as a joint venture with the US company, General Motors. Hyundai at Ulsan has designed and produced its own car, the 'Pony', which it has exported world-

Figure C Progress in South Korea

Indicator	1970	1990
Population (millions)	28	44
Birth rate (per thousand)	45	16
Death rate (per thousand)	16	6
Infant mortality (per thousand live births)	60	23
Life expectancy at birth (years)	52	71
GNP per person (US $)	220	4400
Ships launched (thousand tonnes)	40	2278
Electricity generated (thousand million kilowatt hours)	16	108
Televisions (thousand)	610	15300

Reasons for South Korea's success

- Massive loans from foreign banks and aid from the USA
- A strong government which has ruthlessly crushed opposition

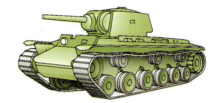

- A cheap labour force (less so since mid-1970s)
- Very hard working, skilled and disciplined labour force
- Use of most modern technology
- Many dynamic business people and managers

wide. By 1987 South Korea produced over 400 000 cars.

Manufacturing now employs 25 per cent of the nation's workforce and earns 35 per cent of the country's income. Agriculture remains important, employing 30 per cent of the workforce and earning 20 per cent of the national income. But there have been problems in South Korea's progress. The country has built up a huge debt to foreign banks. World demand for ships and steel has fallen since the 1970s. The economy is overdependent upon exports, especially to the USA. The government is a form of dictatorship with strict censorship and a ban on opposition. Western governments are placing more restrictions on the imports of manufactured goods. This has encouraged South Korean companies to open factories in the West, for example, a car components plant at Toronto and an electronics plant in Alabama.

It has been forecast that South Korea will be among the world's 15 richest nations by the year 2000. The country has applied for membership of the Organisation of Economic Co-operation and Development (OECD) which until now has been limited to developed countries. South Korea is looking ahead to the twenty-first century when it intends to be a developed country.

QUESTIONS

1 Where is South Korea?

2 a) Copy the map of South Korea (Figure A).
   b) Draw bars on the map proportional to the size of population of the country's major cities as shown in the table below. Draw a key bar, and let 1 centimetre represent 1 million population. (Pusan has been drawn on Figure A as an example.)

Population of South Korean cities

City	Pop (millions)	City	Pop (millions)
Seoul	8.5	Kwangju	0.8
Pusan	3.2	Taejon	0.7
Taegu	1.7	Ulsan	0.5
Inchon	1.1	Masan	0.4

3 List five facts to show that South Korea has made rapid economic and social progress since 1970.

4 Study the table below:

The growth of South Korea's shipbuilding industry

Year	1973	1974	1975	1976	1977	1978	1979
Tonnage launched (thousands)	44	563	582	461	435	528	588
Year	1980	1981	1982	1983	1984	1985	1986
Tonnage launched (thousands)	626	1207	1531	1140	2394	2764	2884

a) Construct a bar graph to illustrate the statistics in the table.
b) Describe the development of the South Korean shipbuilding industry.

5 a) Account for the success of South Korea's 'economic miracle'.
b) What problems has the economic miracle caused for South Korea?

7.6 Is industry the answer?

Most developing countries have modern manufacturing industries. The introduction of industry brings many advantages for a country, but an increasing number of people wonder whether industry brings more problems than benefits.

Figure A The world's financial crisis – how it developed and what might happen

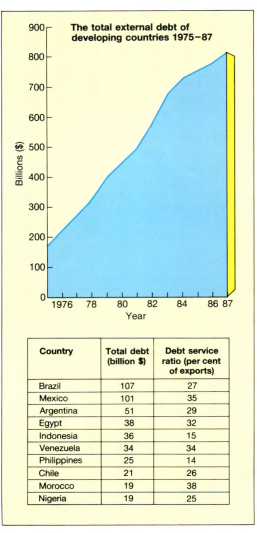

Figure B The graph (top) shows the total external debt of the developing countries, 1975–87, the table shows the leading debtor nations in 1987

Country	Total debt (billion $)	Debt service ratio (per cent of exports)
Brazil	107	27
Mexico	101	35
Argentina	51	29
Egypt	38	32
Indonesia	36	15
Venezuela	34	34
Philippines	25	14
Chile	21	26
Morocco	19	38
Nigeria	19	25

One of the biggest problems is that large-scale manufacturing industry needs a great deal of money. Not simply money to build the factory but also money to supply the expensive infrastructure which modern industry needs, such as electricity, telephones, roads, water and sewage mains. Most of the developing countries are poor and can only obtain this money from outsiders in the developed world. The loans have to be repaid, with interest. Many loans were taken out during the 1970s when interest rates were low and hopes were high. Now the high hopes have turned to despair. Since the late 1970s interest rates in the developed world have risen to high rates and it has become very difficult for developing countries to afford to repay even the interest. Many developing countries are now deeply in dept (Figure B). An increasing amount of their Gross Domestic Product is spent on interest payments. Banks in the developed world are owed over $700 billion by developing countries.

The growth of industry has been accompanied in many places by exploitation of the workforce. They are paid little and work in dangerous, unhealthy conditions. If they fall ill they are discarded without welfare and replaced from the vast number of unemployed. Children are especially exploited.

Building factories has sometimes put many local craftsmen out of work. An automated textile factory, for example, will produce large quantities of cloth by machine, employing few people. Hundreds of weavers may lose their living as the cheaper factory produced textiles flood the market.

The machines produced by modern industry are expensive and complicated. When they break down there may be no skilled repairer available, or no spare parts.

Appropriate technology

The latest high-technology machinery is not suitable for much of the developing world. It is of little use to give people lorries to carry their heavy loads: there may be no suitable roads, no petrol and no mechanics. It is more appropriate to give such people a well made cart which can be pulled by an ox.

Animal power

Oxen are making a comeback in Sierra Leone where farmers can no longer afford to keep machinery like tractors running.

Fuel is scarce and expensive, spare parts are costly and once they break down tractors are likely to stay out of action for long periods of time.

But many of today's farmers have little idea of how to use oxen for ploughing. So a Work Oxen project has been launched, with financial backing from several Western governments, which involves training farmers in the methods and practices of their ancestors.

New Internationalist November 1987

Figure C Extract

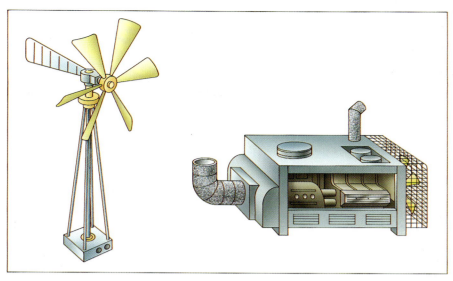

Figure D Water-pumping equipment – wind-powered and diesel-powered

This is an example of appropriate technology, developments suited to the needs and skills of the people. The money spent on buiding mechanized textile factories which put local craftsmen out of work would have been better spent on providing the craftsmen with better designed handlooms.

Appropriate technology may not be very spectacular, but it holds out better hope for real progress in many developing countries. Vast sums of money are not needed for appropriate technology. It uses less energy and causes less pollution.

QUESTIONS

1 Why is the development of manufacturing industry very expensive?
2 a) From where do developing countries obtain the money needed for industrial development?
  b) Why are many developing countries now in debt?
3 Study Figure A and say why the developing world's growing debt poses a threat to the developed world's banking systems and economies.
4 How can the building of a factory in a developing country cause more unemployment than the jobs it creates?
5 Study the two machines in Figure D.
  a) List the advantages and disadvantages of both.
  b) Which would be most appropriate to manufacture in a developing country?
6 'Appropriate technology may not be very spectacular, but it holds out better hope for real progress in many developing countries.' Why is this?

Unit 7 ASSESSMENT

1. a) Describe the situation of Singapore. (3 marks)
   b) How has Singapore's situation assisted its economic growth? (3 marks)
2. a) How wide is Singapore, at its widest point? (1 mark)
   b) What is the area of Singapore? (1 mark)
   c) What is the population of Singapore? (1 mark)
   d) What is the population density of Singapore? (1 mark)
3. What evidence in the article suggests that Singapore is an example of a Newly Industrialized Country? (4 marks)
4. a) As an NIC, what advantages does Singapore have as a location for multi-national manufacturing companies? (4 marks)
   b) What advantages and disadvantages do multi-national companies bring to developing countries? (6 marks)

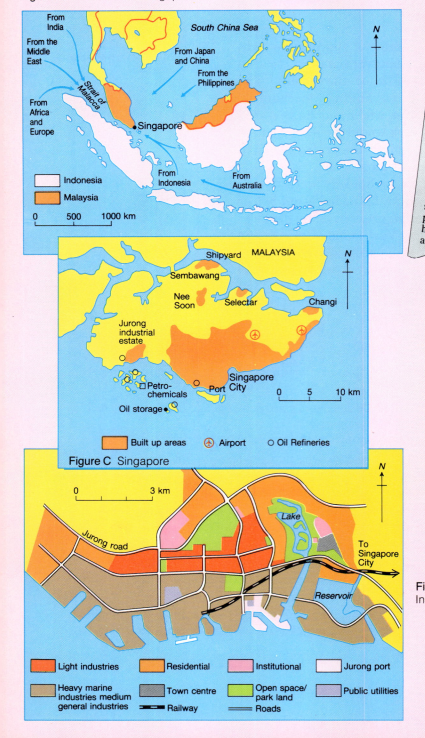

Figure A The location of Singapore

Figure C Singapore

Figure B Extract

Singapore – new industrial giant of the east

Singapore is one of the wealthiest developing countries. Its growth has been based upon trade and, increasingly, upon manufacturing industry. Singapore developed several industries associated with its large seaport such as oil refining, timber processing and shipbuilding. Light electronic industries developed during the 1960s including televisions, radios and tape recorders. Multinational companies rushed to locate new factories in Singapore to make the most of Singapore's advantages to supply the booming demands of people in the developed world. A huge industrial estate was opened at Jurong with a new deepwater port. Over 80 000 people work in 600 factories producing electronics, cameras, soft drinks, cables and many other consumer goods.
The Singapore government wants to move on from the low skill/low paid manufacturing because this mainly involves assembling components imported from elsewhere. The government wants new factories to build the components in Singapore itself. Another aim is to develop more high technology products such as computers, computer peripherals and video recorders. These require more skilled and higher paid labour.

Figure D Singapore – basic information

Area	580 sq. km.
Population	2.53 million
Population density	4360 per sq. km.
Birth rate	16 per thousand
Death rate	5 per thousand
GDP	$17 848 million
GDP per capita	$7 083
Average annual growth rate of GDP	7.6 per cent
Main exports	Rubber, petroleum products, machinery
Main imports	Rubber, machinery, textiles, crude oil

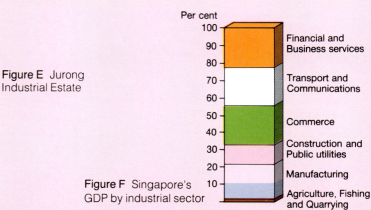

Figure E Jurong Industrial Estate

Figure F Singapore's GDP by industrial sector

5 a) What does GDP mean? (1 mark)
b) What percentage of Singapore's GDP is contributed by (i) primary industry (ii) manufacturing (iii) commerce and financial and business services? (3 marks)
c) 'Singapore's economy has a broader base than many NICs.'
  (i) Do you agree with this statement? Give your reasons. (3 marks)
  (ii) What advantages do you think this broader base has for Singapore's economy? (5 marks)

6 a) (i) Where are Singapore's oil and petro-chemical plants located? (1 mark)
  (ii) What is the main advantage of this location rather than the northern shore of the island? (2 marks)
b) Where is the new Jurong industrial estate located? (1 mark)
c) Describe the main features of the layout of the Jurong industrial estate. (5 marks)
d) List four factories found on the Jurong industrial estate. (2 marks)

7 a) How does the Singapore government want Singapore's industry to develop in the future? (2 marks)
b) What advantages would these new developments bring to Singapore? (4 marks)

8 Study the table below:

Singapore's exports

Country	$ million	Per cent of total
USA	4080	25.1
Japan	1930	11.9
Malaysia	1856	11.4
Indonesia	1710	10.5
EC	1680	10.3
Hong Kong	1025	?
Others	3995	?
Total	16276	100.0

a) Calculate the percentages for Hong Kong and Others. (2 marks)
b) Draw a proportional bar to show all the percentages. (7 marks)

9 a) What is meant by the term 'appropriate technology'? (2 marks)
b) Give two examples of appropriate technology. (2 marks)
c) What are the advantages of appropriate technology to a poor country? (4 marks)

TOTAL: 40 marks

Details for pupil profile sheet Unit 7

Knowledge and understanding

1 Primary product
2 Newly Industrialized Countries
3 The Pacific Basin
4 The debt burden of developing countries
5 Gross Domestic Product
6 Appropriate technology
7 The role of multi-national companies

Skills

1 Draw proportional bars
2 Calculating percentages
3 Draw a bar graph
4 Mark countries on an outline map, using atlas
5 Reading a scatter graph
6 Draw proportional bars on an outline map

Values

1 Awareness of the cause and effects of debt
2 Awareness of the exploitation of people by industry, including European and US multi-nationals, in developing countries
3 An awareness of the constraints on industrial development in developing countries

8.1 Swindon's early growth

Unit 8: Selling Swindon by the pound

To many motorists speeding along the M4 motorway, Swindon is a name on a road sign, an expanse of housing covering a low hill and a collection of colourful factories with foreign sounding names. This town of 140 000 people looks strangely out of place in the Wiltshire countryside, sprawling across a clay vale between the Cotswold Hills and the Marlborough Downs. Swindon provides an excellent study of the changing fortunes of an industrial town.

Swindon's growth has been strongly rooted in its geography. The first people to settle there were probably Saxons during the eighth century. They were attracted by the limestone hill rising above the clay vale which offered a good defensive site. Springs provided a regular water supply and a good variety of soils allowed a range of farming types. Swindon was at first a farming village. By the thirteenth century it was a small market town and by the sixteenth century limestone quarries provided the first industrial jobs.

The transport revolution of the early nineteenth century caused Swindon to change from a small market town into a bustling industrial centre. Swindon was in the right place at the right time, located on the route between London and Bristol. A canal was opened in 1820 linking the River Thames with the River Avon. Fifteen years later the London to Bristol line of the Great Western Railway was built.

Swindon and the railways

Sheds were built at Swindon station to house locomotives and a second line was opened linking Swindon with Cheltenham. The railway junction encouraged the railway company to choose Swindon as the site for its locomotive works in 1841. The choice of the actual site was made in an odd way: the surveyor threw his sandwich over his shoulder and the spot where it landed was where the building of the works was begun!

The Railway Works changed the face of Swindon for ever. Within six years the population doubled from 2000 to 4000. The GWR built a new town of terraced stone cottages for its workers (Figure B). By 1864 there were 2500 people working at the Railway Works and the population of Swindon had reached 7287. Over the next few decades the growth of both the Railway Works and the town was meteoric (Figure C). The demand for houses was so great that the high standards of the early cottages could not be maintained and thousands of brick terrace houses sprawled over the Wiltshire fields. Thousands of steam locomotives were built and repaired at Swindon. People moved to Swindon for work, many from South Wales and Northern England.

Figure A Swindon in the 1840s

Figure B Terraced houses in the Railway Village, Swindon

Swindon was a boom town, but its boom was based on just one source of employment. In 1931 62 per cent of the town's workforce (14 900 people) were employed by the GWR. Most other jobs depended upon servicing the railway works or its employees. The one-industry town was common in Britain's industrial revolution. Crewe and Shildon were other examples of railway towns; Merthyr Tydfil, Consett and Corby were iron and steel towns; Elland and Dewsbury were woollen towns; Colne and Burnley were cotton towns. But in the same way that the growth of an industry brought prosperity, the decline of that industry could bring disaster.

During the 1930s the world entered a serious economic recession. As British industry declined, there was less demand for rail transport. Swindon was badly hit. Thousands of men were laid off from the Railway Works. Hundreds left the town to find work in the new car and engineering factories of Oxford, Gloucester and South-East England. After a century of rapid growth the population of Swindon fell by 4 per cent between 1931 and 1937. The future of the town seemed threatened, it was too closely linked to the success of the railways. The railways were threatened not just by the recession but by increasing competition from road transport. It was clear that the boom days of the railways were over.

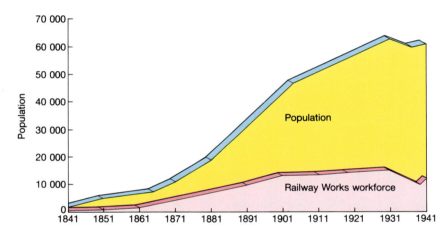

Figure C The population of Swindon and the size of the Railway Works workforce 1841–1941

QUESTIONS

1 Describe (i) the site and (ii) the situation of Swindon.

2 How did Swindon's situation contribute to its rapid growth during the nineteenth century?

3 Study the photograph of the Railway Village (Figure B).
   a) Describe the appearance of the houses.
   b) Why do you think that the later workers' houses were not built to such a high standard?

4 a) What was the population of Swindon in (i) 1841 (ii) 1901 (iii) 1931 (iv) 1937?
   b) Explain the changes in the population between those four years.

5 a) What is meant by a 'one-industry town'?
   b) Name four examples.
   c) What problems does a one-industry town face?
   d) How might these problems be overcome?

8.2 The fastest growing town in Western Europe?

Look at Figure A. How has the one-industry town threatened by the decline of its industrial base been transformed into the 'focal point of Britain's fastest-growing commercial, high-tech developments'?

At the end of the Second World War, Swindon Borough Council considered the future. Altghough several aircraft factories had been built near the town during the war it was obvious that Swindon would have to depend upon the Railway Works as its main employer. The council was determined that the problems of the 1930s would not be allowed to happen again. What could they do?

The council decided that attack was the best form of defence. They decided to try to attract more industry to Swindon and aimed to make the town much larger. A vital decision was that made to buy large areas of farmland around the town using ratepayers money. As land prices rose the council had money and land ownership rights on their side. At first progress was slow, but in 1952 came the Town Development Act. This set up Expanded Towns to take overspill population from London. Faced with the damage of German air raids

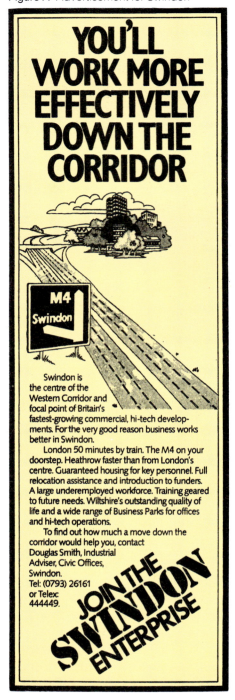

Figure A Advertisement for Swindon

Figure B Swindon's impressive central shopping area

and the problems of congestion and rapid population growth, planners wanted to move people out of London to other towns. Swindon grabbed the chance. Thousands of houses were built in Swindon to house Londoners. Industrial estates were built to house new industry. In 1954 a car body plant was opened. Between 1954 and 1964 over 15 000 new industrial jobs were attracted to Swindon. The town's population began to grow rapidly again (Figure D).

The year 1970 saw the peak of manufacturing jobs in Swindon – over 35 000. Since then the number of manufacturing jobs has declined by 13 000 but over 20 000 jobs in service and distribution industries have been created. Since 1945 the population of Swindon has more than doubled from 65 000 to 140 000.

Since 1978 Swindon has had to fight even harder for the new jobs it needs. This is because government policy has changed. The overspill policy is now a thing of the past. Government and private resources are being concentrated in the inner cities such as the London docklands. Swindon now has less money available to spend on industrial development because the government has reduced its payments to high spending councils. Nearly all of the council's 'land bank' has now been sold. Despite this, new jobs have still been attracted including many in high-tech manufacturing and research.

As Swindon has grown the council has built a vast new shopping centre, new schools, a new sixth form college, a theatre and two leisure centres. The old railway town has changed out of all recognition. The Railway Works finally closed in 1986. Only the Railway Museum and the restored Railway Village remind Swindonians of their town's industrial beginnings.

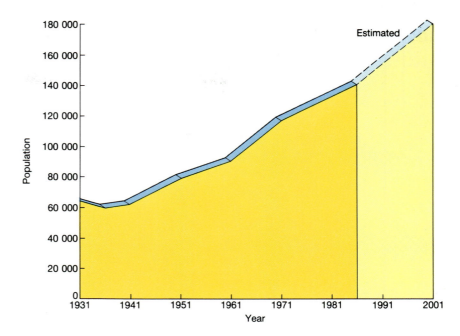

Figure D The population of Swindon 1931–2001

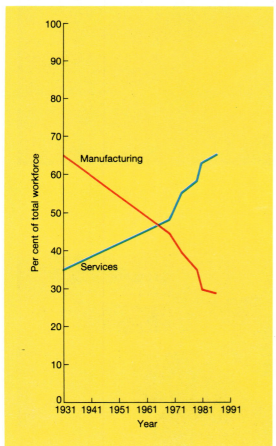

Figure C Manufacturing and service employment in Swindon 1931–1986

QUESTIONS

1. Look at Figure A.
   a) What is the corridor referred to in the advertisement?
   b) Make a table showing the advantages of Swindon as a location for industry using the following headings:
   Transport, Labour, Sites, Housing, Environment.
   c) 'Find out how much a move down the corridor would help you'. From where does this suggest that Swindon expects to receive new companies?
2. How did the population of Swindon change between 1941 and 1985?
3. Why did Swindon Borough Council buy large areas of farmland around the town after 1945?
4. How did the Town Development Act help Swindon?
5. How has the nature of employment in Swindon changed since 1970?
6. Why has Swindon had to fight even harder for new jobs since 1978?

8.3 The industry of the future?

The photographs show views of one of Britain's most futuristic industrial estates. This is the Windmill Hill Business Park at Swindon.

Windmill Hill has been developed by a London-based company which is backed by money from Kuwait. It is claimed to be Britain's first integrated business park. Windmill Hill has been built in six phases between 1984 and 1990. The farmland on which the business park is built has been landscaped to create an undulating 35 hectare site with over 50 000 newly planted trees and an ornamental pool. The centrepiece of the business park is the windmill itself. It looks as if it has been on the site a long while, but in fact it was moved stone by stone from its original site on the Wiltshire Downs and rebuilt. This is a remarkable example of the expense to which property developers are prepared to go to provide an attractive working environment.

Figure A Two views of Windmill Hill. Notice the car parking space close to each building, and the landscaping

Figure B Advertisement for Windmill Hill

Each building at Windmill Hill has a unique design. Each one is clad in reflective glass, and has air conditioning, a highly flexible interior layout and raised floors for computers. There is ample car parking space.

Windmill Hill aims to provide an excellent location for company headquarters, research and development establishments and high-tech industry.

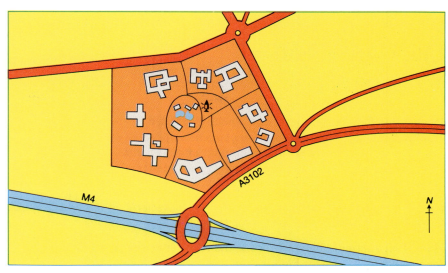

Figure C Windmill Hill Business Park

Among the first companies to choose Windmill Hill are a US company manufacturing semi-conductors and the headquarters of a US-based credit card company which moved down the Western Corridor from Reading to Swindon. When complete the business park will include shops, cash dispensers, sports facilities and a restaurant.

QUESTIONS

1 Describe the appearance of the buildings in the photographs.

2 Study the advertisement for Windmill Hill (Figure B).
   a) How far is Windmill Hill from the M4 motorway? Why is this likely to be an advantage for companies wishing to locate at the business park?
   b) What other locational advantages does the advertisement stress?

3 a) What has been done to make the environment of the business park attractive?
   b) Why do you think the property developers have gone to so much expense to make the environment attractive?
   c) Why do the buildings at Windmill Hill have raised floors?

4 Make a copy of the map of Windmill Hill and add the following labels in the correct places:
   A3102 dual carriageway link with M4
   M4 motorway
   Junction 16
   To Heathrow Airport and London
   To Bristol and Bath
   To Swindon town centre
   Ornamental pool
   Windmill

5 a) What are the advantages of a location on an industrial estate?
   b) What type of industry has been attracted to Windmill Hill?

Unit 8 ASSESSMENT

It is possible to work out the degree of industrial localization for a particular area if we have detailed employment statistics. The *location quotient* helps us to see the relative importance of various occupations in an area.

A location quotient is worked out using the following simple formula:

$$\frac{\text{location}}{\text{quotient}} = \frac{\%\ \text{of area X's employment in employment sector Y}}{\%\ \text{of UK's employment in employment sector Y}}$$

A location quotient above 1.0 means that the percentage for the particular area is higher than that for the whole country.

Study the table below which shows employment statistics for Swindon. If we take the employment sector of Agriculture we see that 1.8% of Swindon's workforce is employed in agriculture compared with 1.7% in the UK as a whole. We can calculate the location quotient for agriculture in Swindon:

$$\text{location quotient} = \frac{1.8\%}{1.7\%} = 1.06$$

Thus there is a slightly higher concentration of agricultural employment in the Swindon area than the national average.

1. a) Copy the table below and complete the location quotients. (8 marks)
   b) Why do you think that the location quotients for Construction and Distribution are so high? (4 marks)

Employment sector	% of Swindon's workforce 1986	% of UK's workforce 1986	Location quotient
Agriculture	1.8	1.7	1.06
TOTAL PRIMARY	1.8	2.9	?
Engineering & vehicles	24.5	11.0	?
Other manufacturing	6.7	15.1	?
TOTAL MANUFACTURING	31.2	26.1	?
Construction	6.8	4.4	?
Distribution	15.6	12.1	?
Office jobs	35.7	38.0	?
Other services	8.9	16.5	?
TOTAL SERVICES	67.0	71.0	?

Figure A Swindon's employment compared with the UK as a whole

2. Study Figure B.
   a) Copy the two proportional bars and complete them using the statistics in the table. (8 marks)
   b) (i) Which employment sector had the highest change between 1971 and 1986? (ii) Why was this? (3 marks)
   c) Why is the manufacturing sector in Swindon declining? (3 marks)

Employment sector	% of Swindon's workforce 1971	% of Swindon's workforce 1986
TOTAL PRIMARY	2.3	1.8
Engineering and vehicles	32.4	24.5
Other manufacturing	12.9	6.7
TOTAL MANUFACTURING	45.3	31.2
Construction	5.0	6.8
Distribution	13.2	15.6
Office jobs	23.0	35.7
Other services	11.2	8.9
TOTAL SERVICES	52.4	67.0

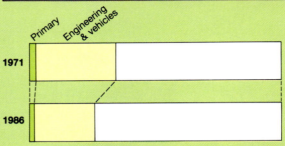

Figure B Changes in Swindon's employment structure 1971–1986

3. Figure C shows the composition of Swindon's population by age and sex.
   a) Copy and complete the age/sex pyramid using the statistics in the table. (10 marks)
   b) Which age group has the highest total percentage of people? (1 mark)
   c) What effect will this have had on Swindon's labour force between 1981 and 1991? (2 marks)
   d) What does this indicate about Swindon's birth rate? (1 mark)

Figure C The composition of Swindon's population by age and sex

Age Group	% Male	% Female
0–9	7.0	6.6
10–19	8.7	8.4
20–29	7.9	7.9
30–39	7.1	6.9
40–49	5.8	5.7
50–59	5.8	5.7
60–69	4.2	4.4
Over 70	3.0	4.9
TOTAL	49.5	50.5

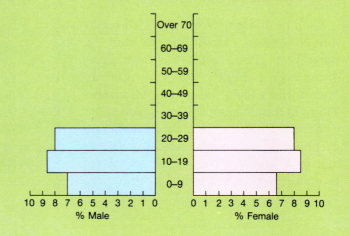

4 Design a poster to advertise the advantages of Swindon as a location for modern industry. (10 marks)

5 Study Figure D.

a) In which period was the largest number of industrial areas built? (1 mark)

b) Describe the location of (i) the pre-1950 industrial areas and (ii) the industrial areas built between 1980 and 1989 in Swindon. (4 marks)

c) Account for the differing locations of these two periods. (4 marks)

d) Using evidence from the map state where you think much of Swindon's recent growth has occurred. (2 marks)

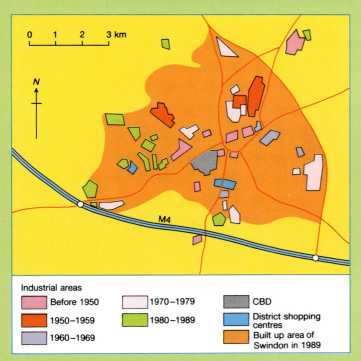

Figure D Industrial areas in Swindon

6 a) Describe with the aid of a sketch map the layout and appearance of the Windmill Hill Business Park. (6 marks)

b) What kind of industry would be especially attracted to Windmill Hill? (2 marks)

c) What advantages does Windmill Hill possess for such industry? (6 marks)

TOTAL: 75 marks

Details for pupil profile sheet Unit 8

Knowledge and understanding

1 One-industry town
2 Effects of economic recession
3 Site and situation
4 Expanded Town
5 Overspill population
6 Business park
7 Location quotient
8 Age/sex pyramid

Skills

1 Interpreting a newspaper advertisement
2 Read a line graph
3 Calculate location quotients
4 Copy and complete a map
5 Draw proportional bars
6 Draw an age/sex pyramid
7 Design a poster
8 Draw a sketch map

Values

1 Awareness of the role of local councils and government in industrial development.

9.1 The geography of unemployment

Unit 9: Post-industrial Britain

Answer question 1 before you read on. Although Figure B suggests that there are much higher rates of unemployment in the north and west of the UK, the map gives only a very general picture. There are areas of low unemployment in northern England and areas of high unemployment in the South-East (Margate in Kent, for example, has had 26 per cent unemployment).

The worst areas of unemployment can be divided into three types. Firstly, depressed areas of inner cities where manufacturing industry has declined. Secondly, industrial towns whose traditional industry has declined, such as Consett where the steelworks closed. Thirdly, seaside resorts where jobs, especially for the young, are limited outside the holiday season.

Figure A shows how average unemployment rates have increased rapidly since the mid-1970s. By 1985 3.3 million people were unemployed. The causes of this dramatic increase include:

- A worldwide recession caused by the increase in oil prices in 1973/74 and again in 1979.

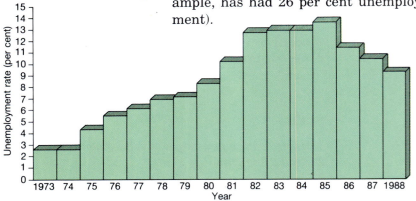

Figure A Unemployment rates in the UK 1973–1988

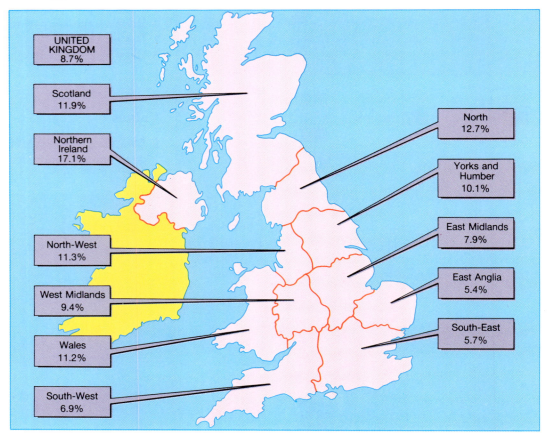

Figure B Unemployment rates in the Regions of the UK

110

- A decrease in demand for several traditional industrial products, particularly iron and steel, coal, ships, woollen and cotton textiles.
- Increased automation and mechanization has reduced the labour demands of many industries.
- Competition from foreign manufacturers, especially in motor vehicles and electronics.
- The policy of the British government which allowed interest rates to increase, so making it difficult for industry to afford to invest in new machinery. The government also allowed the international value of the pound to rise so high that British goods became very expensive overseas, so cutting British exports.
- The failure of British industry to adopt new manufacturing methods, and the increasingly high wage rates demanded by the workforce without increases in productivity.

Since 1985 the unemployment total has fallen, but the days of full employment have clearly passed. Many people have said that Britain has moved on a stage in its economic development. They say that Britain has now entered a 'post-industrial' period. By this they really mean 'post-manufacturing'. Service industries have continued to grow despite the recession. Less than one-third of the British workforce is now employed in manufacturing.

Figure C These unemployed people are working on Operation Eyesore in Bradford, a government-funded scheme to provide useful community work

Figure D Regional unemployment and pay rates. The figures show the ratio of regional pay and unemployment to the national average (100%)

Region	Pay	Unemployment	Rank Pay	Rank unemployment
London	113.1	82.5	1	?
North	100.4	146.5	2	?
North-West	100.0	123.7	3	?
South-East	99.0	69.3	4	?
Scotland	98.8	118.4	5	?
West Midlands	98.6	119.3	6	?
Wales	98.3	125.4	7	?
Yorks & Humberside	97.8	115.8	8	?
East Midlands	97.5	95.6	9	?
East Anglia	95.2	71.8	10	?
South-West	95.1	88.6	11	?
Northern Ireland	89.8	161.5	12	?
National average	100.0	100.0		

QUESTIONS

1. Figure B shows the unemployment rates in the regions of the UK.
   a) On an outline map of the UK draw in the regional boundaries shown on Figure B.
   b) Shade in the regions according to this colour key:

Unemployment rate	Colour
6.9% and under	WHITE
7–9.9%	YELLOW
10–12.9%	ORANGE
13% and above	RED

   Add the colour key to your map.
   You have drawn a *choropleth* map. The intensity of the unemployment is shown by the darkening colours from white for lowest through to red for highest.
   c) Which four regions have unemployment rates below the national average?
   d) Which five regions have the highest levels of unemployment?
   e) How could you describe the geography of unemployment in the UK using the terms North, South, East, and West?
2. Why does Figure B only give a very general picture of unemployment in the regions of the UK?
3. Explain why the following three areas may suffer high unemployment:
   a) inner cities b) traditional industrial towns c) seaside resorts.
4. Explain how the following factors have contributed to unemployment in the UK:
   a) changing demand for industrial products b) automation
   c) government policy d) foreign competition.
5. a) Copy Figure D and rank the regions in terms of unemployment.
   b) It has been suggested that some areas have 'priced themselves out of employment' through high wage levels. Does the completed table lend any support to this suggestion?

9.2 Government aid

Government policy has become an important influence on the location of industry in Britain during the twentieth century. Before the 1920s the government had ignored the question of industrial location. This had been left to the industrial companies themselves. While Britain's economy had been growing this policy was safe enough for the government. However, during the 1920s the economy suffered a recession. The effects of the recession were especially bad in those regions where traditional industries such as coal, steel and shipbuilding declined. Unemployment rates were very high in these regions, yet elsewhere in Britain, especially in the South-East and the Midlands, new industries were growing rapidly and there was little unemployment.

It was in 1928 that the government made its first moves towards helping the unemployed. The Industrial Transfer Act tried to persuade the unemployed to move to areas where work was available. This had some success, but most people were unwilling to leave their homes and their friends. This policy was known as 'moving the workers to the work'. It was in 1934 that the reverse policy, 'moving work to the workers', was begun, and this type of policy has continued ever since.

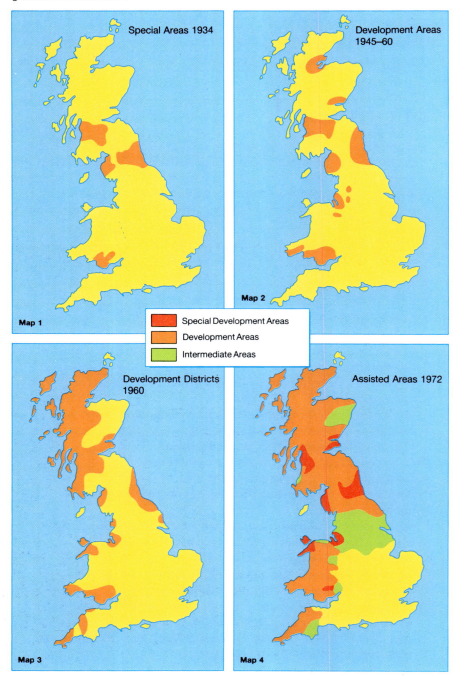

Figure A The history of government assistance

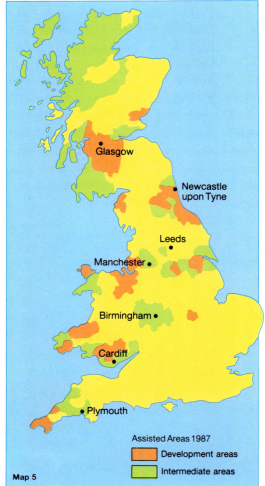

1934: The Special Areas Act set up the four areas shown on Map 1 to receive grants and loans to encourage new industry to move there. South Wales, North-East England, West Cumberland and Clydeside all faced high unemployment as their traditional industries declined. One notable success of this policy was the building of a new steelworks at Ebbw Vale in 1938.

1945: The Distribution of Industry Act created the modern Development Area policy and extended the areas to be given assistance (Map 2).

1947: The Town & Country Planning Act forced companies to obtain an Industrial Development Certificate (IDC) if they wanted to expand. IDCs were not normally given outside Development Areas.

1960: The Local Employment Act expanded the Development Areas (Map 3).

1967: Special Development Areas with higher rates of grants and other allowances were set up by the Industry Act.

1972: The Industry Act expanded the Development and Special Development Areas, and introduced Intermediate Areas with a lower level of assistance.

1978: The Inner Urban Areas Act made the inner areas of Britain's major conurbations, including inner London, eligible for assistance similar to the Development Areas.

1982: The size of the assisted areas was greatly reduced (Map 5). Enterprise Zones were introduced. These are small areas where planning controls are relaxed and no rates need be paid for ten years.

1984: Freeports were established. Firms within the freeports have to pay no taxes or customs duties on goods imported and assembled into finished products which are then exported.

1985: Development and Special Development Areas replaced by Development Areas. Intermediate Areas remain, but assistance reduced. West Midlands made an Intermediate Area.

Until 1982 government policy had progressively increased the areas for assistance until about 47 per cent of Britain's working population was within an assisted area. Since 1982 the percentage has fallen to 27 per cent. This reflects the government's concern that regional aid was an expensive way of providing jobs and that it is more effective to concentrate assistance in the worst affected places. At the same time it has abandoned the idea of limiting growth in those areas outside the assisted areas.

Figure B Employment changes by Region

Region	Manufacturing employment (percentage change)	Total employment (percentage change)
South-East	−25	+ 2
East Anglia	− 3	+13
South-West	−15	+ 5
West Midlands	−29	− 7
East Midlands	−18	+ 1
Yorks & Humberside	−35	− 6
North-West	−35	−12
North	−34	−10
Wales	−36	−13
Scotland	−38	− 8
Northern Ireland	−33	n.a.

QUESTIONS

1 a) When did the British government make its first moves towards helping the unemployed?
   b) What was the policy first adopted?

2 a) How did government policy change in 1934?
   b) Name the first four regions to be assisted.

3 What do you understand by the following:
   a) Development Area b) Intermediate Area c) Enterprise Zone d) Freeport?

4 How and why has government regional policy changed since 1982?

5 Study Figure B
   a) Does the table suggest that the regional development policy is working? Give your reasons.
   b) What factors may be responsible for (i) the success of the four regions which have increased their total employment and (ii) the failure of the six regions which have lost employment?
   c) What may be the effects of growth or decrease in the workforce of a region?

9.3 The EC regional policy

The European Community has been called 'a rich nations' club'. It is certainly true that several of the EC countries are amongst the richest in the world. However, the contrast between the rich and poor within the EC is surprisingly great (Figure A). The richest EC nation, Denmark, has a GDP per capita nearly five times higher than the poorest EC nation, Portugal.

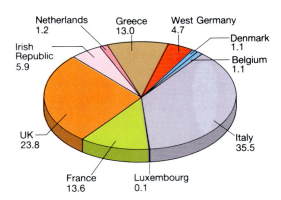

Figure C National quotas for the ERDF (per cent), 1985

Regional contrasts within the countries of the EC are also very great. Even rich Denmark has regions which are relatively poor with high unemployment rates and lack of opportunities. Figure B shows the contrasts across the regions of the EC.

In 1975 the EC established the European Regional Development Fund (ERDF). It is intended to help the national governments assist underde-

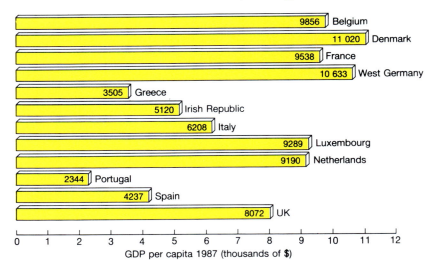

Figure A (*above*) Rich and poor nations in the EC, 1987

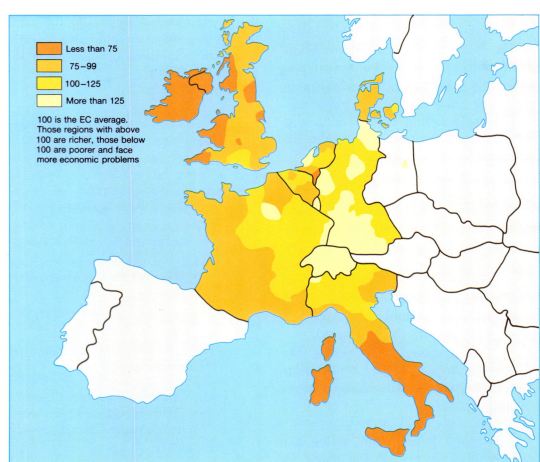

Figure B The relative intensity of regional problems in the EC, 1977–81

veloped regions. Four criteria are used to identify such regions:
1 Those where GDP is below the national average.
2 Those with an above average dependence on agriculture or declining industry.
3 Those with a high unemployment rate.
4 Those with net emigration of the local population.

Under the ERDF national governments define their assisted areas, and all applications for ERDF aid are passed on to the EC via the national government. Ninety-five per cent of the Fund is distributed on the basis of national quotas (Figure C). The remaining 5 per cent of the Fund is used to aid areas which have suffered as the result of EC policies, such as the closure of iron and steelworks under the EC's restructuring programme.

Between 1975 and 1984 the UK received over £1200 million from the ERDF, of which two thirds went on infrastructural projects such as the construction of the Kielder Water reservoir which received £37 million. Industrial projects helped by the ERDF include the construction of the Ford engine plant at Bridgend which received £10 million.

The ERDF was very small in 1975, amounting to only 4.8 per cent of the total EC budget. It has grown slowly since then to 10 per cent of the total budget by 1987, but it is still very small in comparison with the CAP which accounts for 70 per cent of the total budget.

There are other EC institutions which assist regional development:
• The European Coal and Steel Community (ECSC) provides cheap loans and grants in areas subject to modernization or closure of their coal or steel industries. For example, £190 million was loaned to British Coal for the new Selby coalfield.
• The European Social Fund (ESF) provides grants for retraining in areas of high unemployment. For example, £4 million was granted to Greater Manchester Council for adult literacy training.
• The European Investment Bank (EIB) provides loans for economic development in the assisted areas. For example, £120 million was loaned to the Central Electricity Generating Board for the Dinorwic pumped-storage power station.

Figure D The Ford engine plant at Bridgend received £10 million from the ERDF

QUESTIONS

1 a) Why has the EC been called 'a rich nations' club'?
   b) Using Figure A to help you, construct a table of the EC nations in rank order of their GDP per capita.

2 Using Figure B to help you, answer the following questions:
   a) Name five of the poorest regions of the UK.
   b) Name five of the poorest regions of the EC outside the UK.
   c) Name the only area of the UK which is above the EC average of 100.
   d) Describe the location of the most prosperous areas shown on the map.
   e) Which is the only country with all its regions above the EC average?

3 a) What is the ERDF?
   b) When was it established?
   c) What is the aim of the ERDF?
   d) How does the ERDF identify underdeveloped regions?

4 How is the ERDF's fund distributed?

5 a) What do the following initials represent (i) ECSC (ii) ESF (iii) EIB?
   b) Give examples of projects assisted by these three organizations, and by the ERDF.

9.4 The leisure boom

Look at the table below (Figure C) showing some changes affecting the average Briton between 1960 and 1986. These figures show that people in Britain have more spare time available. During the same period people have become richer as average incomes have risen. Much of the spare time and extra money is spent on leisure activities at home (Figure D). Much leisure time is also spent on activities outside the home. Leisure now accounts for 28 per cent of all consumer spending.

The growth in demand for leisure activities has fuelled the growth of the 'leisure industry'. Some people have attacked leisure jobs. They say they are not 'real jobs'. But over two million people now have jobs connected with leisure – that's one in ten of all workers! There are problems with leisure jobs: up to 50 per cent are only seasonal and many are low paid, unskilled jobs. However, more skilled, higher paid jobs are becoming more common as the leisure industry expands.

Figure F shows the most popular destinations for leisure visitors in Britain. Tourists and day-trippers are attracted to historic sites, museums, zoos and wildlife parks, seaside resorts, theme parks and sporting events. Such locations are sometimes called 'honeypots' because they attract human visitors like a honeypot attracts bees. The

Figure A Stonehenge – a 'honeypot' which has suffered from too many visitors

Figure B Heritage Coasts and major seaside resorts in England and Wales

Figure D The results of a survey of British families' leisure activities at home

- The average annual family spending on leisure at home is £1800
- 16 hours per week is spent watching television
- 31 per cent of families watch a video film at least once a week
- 34 per cent of families eat a takeaway meal at least once a week
- 57 per cent of families play cards or a board game at least once a week

Figure C Some indicators of social change in Britain

Indicator	1960	1986
Average working week (hours)	48	43
Average paid holiday (days)	10	24
Unemployment	346 000	3 300 000
Average life expectancy (years)	69	76

Figure E The planned Wonderworld theme park at Corby

most popular honeypot of all is Blackpool beach which attracts up to 7 million visitors a year.

Figure E sums up the changing nature of the British economy. The pleasure theme park shown is Wonderworld at Corby in Northamptonshire. The park is to be built on derelict land which, until the 1970s, was used for quarrying iron ore to supply Corby's iron and steel works which closed in 1980 with the loss of 7000 jobs.

Figure F The number of visitors to the honeypots

Tourist attraction	Visitors (millions per year)
Blackpool beach	7.0
British Museum	3.2
Science Museum	3.1
National Gallery	2.7
Tower of London	2.4
National History Museum	2.4
Madame Tussaud's	2.1
Alton Towers	2.0
London Zoo	1.2
Kew Gardens	1.1
Windsor Castle	1.0
Roman Baths, Bath	0.9
Stonehenge	0.9
Edinburgh Castle	0.8

QUESTIONS

1. a) How did the average working week and paid holiday change between 1960 and 1986?
   b) What effect have these changes had upon leisure time?
2. a) How many people in Britain are employed in leisure?
   b) How have leisure jobs been criticized?
3. a) What do you understand by the term 'tourist honeypot'?
   b) Name the four most popular leisure attractions in Britain.
   c) What do you think are the most popular leisure attractions in your area?
4. Figure A shows Stonehenge.
   a) How many people visit Stonehenge each year?
   b) What are the attractions of Stonehenge?
   c) What problems are created by the large number of visitors?
   d) What evidence is there from the photograph of the measures taken to control visitors?
5. Figure B shows the most important seaside resorts in Britain.
   a) Copy the map.
   b) Name the seaside resorts using your atlas to help you.
   c) Why are most of the resorts in southern Britain?
   d) What type and time of day will see most pressure on seaside resorts?
   e) How can seaside resorts overcome problems of tourist pressure?
   f) What do you think the stretches of Heritage Coast are?
6. a) Over the period of a week, record the amount of leisure time you had and the leisure activities which you were engaged in.
   b) What was the total length of time you spent on leisure activities over the week?
   c) Which two leisure activities did you spend most time on?
   d) How much of your leisure time was spent (i) indoors and (ii) outdoors?
   e) How are your leisure activities affected by the weather and the time of year?
   f) How do your findings compare with those listed in Figure D for the 'average' British family?

9.5 Leisure in the countryside

Figure C shows the National Parks of England and Wales and the National Scenic Areas of Scotland. These are some of the nation's most attractive areas of countryside. Britain is one of the most densely populated countries in the world, so it is not surprising that these areas of countryside are under great pressure from tourists.

National Parks were set up following the National Parks and Access to the Countryside Act of 1949. This marked the end of a long period of pressure from organisations such as the Council for the Preservation of Rural England (CPRE). Twelve National Parks were suggested of which the ten shown on Figure A were designated as National Parks between 1950 and 1957. The two suggestions not designated were the South Downs and East Anglia; this meant that all the National Parks were in highland Britain, well away from the densely populated industrial areas of the Midlands and the South-East. However, in 1986 the government announced that the Norfolk Broads would become a National Park in 1988. This reflected the rapidly increasing tourist pressure on the Broads which has threatened to destroy this fragile area of lakes and waterways.

National Parks are *not* open-air museums owned by the government, nor are they a playground preserved for tourists. National Parks *are* simply areas considered by the government to be of national importance in environmental quality.

Figure A Land ownership of the Lake District National Park

Landowner	Per cent of total area
Private individuals and organisations	62.8
National Trust	22
NW Water Authority	7
Forestry Commission	5
National Park Authority	3
Ministry of Defence	0.2

Figure B Milford Haven, including part of the Pembrokeshire Coast National Park – the threat from the oil industry

Figure C National Parks and National Scenic Areas

National Park Authorities

Each National Park has a Park Authority established by Act of Parliament. The Authority consists of local councillors and members appointed by the government. Each Authority has a staff of professionals including planners, wardens and environmental scientists. The Authority has a number of functions:

- It acts as the local planning authority, controlling new developments in order to preserve the natural landscape.
- It protects wildlife and places of interest.
- It provides access to the general public and provides facilities and information for visitors.

Land ownership in the National Parks

The creation of a National Park does not affect the ownership of land. Most of the land in the National Parks is owned by farmers, private landowners and organizations such as the Forestry Commission, the regional water authorities and the National Trust (a charity which owns many beauty spots and historic buildings). Figure A shows the land ownership of the Lake District National Park.

Problems facing the National Parks

The National Parks are under great pressure from tourists. For example, about one-third of Britain's population is within day-trip distance of the Peak District National Park and over 8 million people visit the Park each year. The tourists can cause many problems:

- traffic congestion
- noise
- litter
- vandalism and unintentional damage
- forest and moorland fires
- erosion of the most heavily used paths

The National Parks are under pressure from other sources as well. Modern farming methods demand changes in the farm buildings and even in the farming landscape. Forestry plantations have been criticized because they feature foreign coniferous trees and because these trees were planted in straight lines in the early days, which looked very out of place.

Industry, especially mining and quarrying, seeks the minerals found in the National Parks, including granite and china clay on Dartmoor, slate in Snowdonia, chalk on the North York Moors and limestone in the Yorkshire Dales.

National Parks are not the only areas of Britain where development is controlled in order to preserve the environment. In Scotland there are National Scenic Areas which are similar in purpose to National Parks. There are also 33 Areas of Outstanding Natural Beauty (AONBs). These cover 10 per cent of the land area of England and Wales. They are not wildscape, like most of the National Parks, but are coastal and agricultural areas. The most scenic coasts are known as Heritage Coasts. Some small areas are of particular biological or geographical interest. They are termed Sites of Special Scientific Interest (SSSIs). There are nearly 4000 SSSIs throughout the UK. Landowners have to seek permission for any change in land use.

The latest conservation/leisure area is the Country Park. Many are recognised by the Countryside Commission, the government body which oversees conservation. The parks were set up by local authorities using government grants. They are small and mostly located in densely populated areas. There are 170 Country Parks throughout the UK.

Figure D Shooting the rapids

QUESTIONS

1 a) Which Act of Parliament set up National Parks in England and Wales?
b) What is a National Park?
c) How many National Parks were established between 1950 and 1957?
d) Describe the general location of these National Parks.
e) Why did the designation of the Norfolk Broads as a National Park mark a difference in the general location of Parks?

2 Make a copy of Figure C on an outline map of Britain. Name the cities shown by their first letters, using an atlas to help you.

3 a) What is a National Park Authority?
b) What are the functions of a Park Authority?

4 a) Draw a pie graph or divided bar graph to illustrate the information in Figure A.
b) What is the National Trust?
c) What is the likely use of the land owned by (i) North-West Water (ii) the Forestry Commission (iii) the Ministry of Defence?

5 Study Figure C and suggest why (i) the Peak District is the most visited National Park by day-trippers and (ii) Snowdonia is the least visited by day-trippers.

6 Discuss the pressures facing the National Parks.

9.6 The Brecon Beacons National Park

The Brecon Beacons National Park in South Wales takes its name from the range of mountains at its centre. It was established in 1957, and covers 1344 square kilometres of open sandstone moorland.

The attractions of the Park

- **Scenery.** Much of the park is underlain by Old Red Sandstone which forms open, hilly moorland rising to nearly 900 metres at Pen y Fan (Figure B). Along the southern edge of the Park narrow bands of Carboniferous Limestone produce dramatically different scenery, with remarkable cave systems and fine waterfalls.

- **Caving.** At Dan-yr-Ogof is a system of spectacular limestone caves open to the general public (Figure A). There are many other cave systems which can be explored by experienced cavers, including Ogof Ffynnon Ddu, the largest known cave system in Britain.

- **Pony-trekking.** There are many trekking centres in the Park which provide half-day, day or week courses.

- **Boating, sailing and canoeing.** Llangorse Lake is the largest lake in South Wales. It is a moraine-dammed lake created during the Ice Age. It is popular for sailing. The Brecon and Montgomery Canal can be used for cruising and canoeing.

- **Fishing.** The River Usk is a famous salmon river. Many of the Park's reservoirs are stocked with trout and the canal and Llangorse Lake offer coarse fishing.

- **Ancient monuments.** There are several prehistoric tombs and standing stones such as Maen Llia (Figure E). Near Brecon is the large Roman fort of Y Gaer. There are several castles, the largest being Carreg Cennen (Figure F).

Figure A (below) Inside the Dan-yr-Ogof Cathedral Cave

Figure B (below right) Pen y Fan

Figure C (below left) Waterfall on the Afon Mellte

Figure D Brecon Beacons National Park

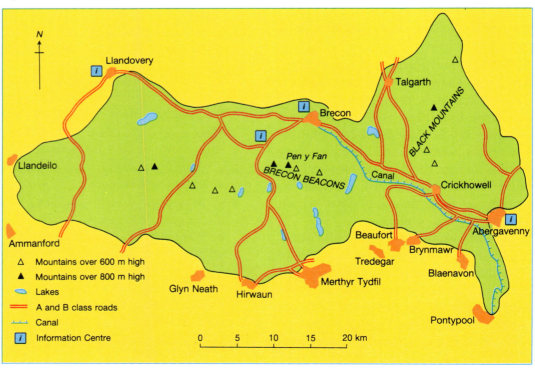

There are a number of small towns and several villages in the National Park. The Park Committee has to consider the interests of the people who live in the Park very carefully. Many of them are farmers anxious to use the land as efficiently as possible. The Park is mainly a farming area. Ninety per cent of the Park is used for farming and 85 per cent of the land is owned by private individuals.

The National Park Committee runs four Information Centres which help people to discover the attractions of the area. A number of National Park wardens are employed to patrol the Park and assist people if required. The Committee also runs a Mountain Centre where displays, talks and films are available. Picnic sites, nature trails and forest walks are provided for visitors.

Although the Brecon Beacons National Park is little threatened by development, there are pressures on the landscape. Many of the area's deep glaciated valleys have been dammed to create reservoirs supplying the industrial cities to the south. There have been proposals to enlarge some of the reservoirs. There are several large coniferous plantations owned by the Forestry Commission. There are several large limestone quarries which scar the landscape, create noise and dust, and require a stream of large lorries to transport the stone. To the north of the Brecon Beacons themselves is an army firing range which shatters the peace of the Park's major walking country. The National Park Committee has to carefully balance the needs of the area's inhabitants and landowners with its main aim to conserve the beauty and peace of this attractive area.

Figure E (*above left*) Maen Llia standing stone

Figure F (*above*) Carreg Cennen Castle

QUESTIONS

1 Where is the Brecon Beacons National Park?

2 You work for the Brecon Beacons National Park Committee. Using a sheet of A4 paper, prepare a brochure setting out the attractions of the National Park for tourists. Your brochure should include simple sketch maps of the Park itself and of the main routes to the Park. Make the brochure itself as colourful, attractive and informative as you can.

3 Describe the pressures facing the Brecon Beacons using the following headings: a) Tourism b) Farming c) Water supply d) Forestry e) Quarrying f) Ministry of Defence.

4 You are a member of the National Park Committee's planning team. With your neighbour you should consider the following proposals for developments in the Brecon Beacons National Park and discuss the suitability of each before deciding which should be allowed to proceed:

a) Opening of a new quarry in the south of the Park which will provide 16 jobs.
b) Building of a silage storage silo at a farm in the east of the Park which will allow the farmer to increase his herd of cattle.
c) Opening of a water-skiing school on Llangorse Lake which will provide 5 new jobs.
d) Construction of a new marina and boat hire centre on the Brecon and Montgomery Canal which will provide 5 new jobs.
e) Widening of the Abergavenny to Brecon road to ease problems of traffic congestion experienced regularly on summer weekends.

Unit 9 ASSESSMENT

1 Study Figure A.
   a) (i) Which region had the highest growth in the employed workforce? (1 mark)
      (ii) Name three other regions which experienced growth in the employed workforce. (3 marks)
   b) (i) Which region had the greatest decrease in the employed workforce? (1 mark)
      (ii) Name five other regions which experienced a decrease in the employed workforce. (5 marks)
      (iii) What factors might explain the decrease in the workforce? (5 marks)
   c) (i) Which region experienced the highest growth in GDP per person? (1 mark)
      (ii) Name four other regions which experienced growth in GDP per person. (4 marks)
   d) (i) Which two regions experienced the greatest decrease in GDP per person? (2 marks)
      (ii) Name three other regions which experienced a decrease in GDP per person. (3 marks)
   e) (i) Which two regions had the highest population increase? (2 marks)
      (ii) Name two other regions whose population increased. (2 marks)
      (iii) Why is the population in these regions increasing? (4 marks)
   f) (i) Which two regions had the greatest population decrease? (2 marks)
      (ii) Name four other regions whose population decreased. (4 marks)
      (iii) Why is the population in these six regions declining? (4 marks)
   g) Does the map suggest that the regional development policy is a great success? Give your reasons. (3 marks)
   h) (i) Which two regions have the highest overall increases? (2 marks)
      (ii) What are the attractions of these regions? (4 marks)

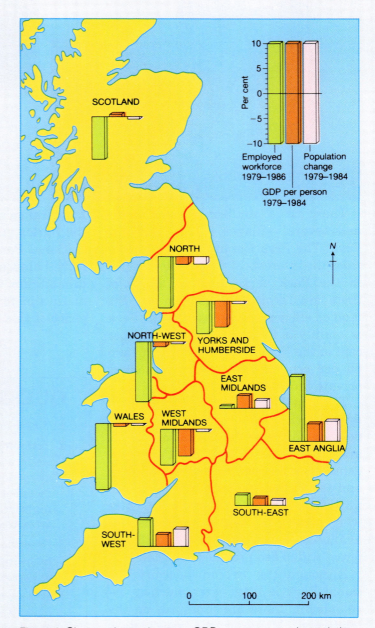

Figure A Changes in employment, GDP per person, and population in the Regions of Britain, 1979–84

2 Study Figure B.
  a) Name the four most popular reasons for making trips into the countryside. (4 marks)
  b) What do you understand by 'Pick your own' farms? (2 marks)
  c) Name one organization which owns historic houses. (1 mark)
  d) What are Country Parks? (2 marks)

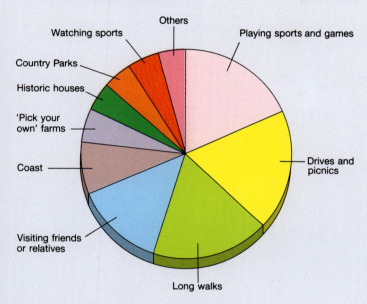

Figure B Reasons for trips to the countryside in Britain (by percentage of population)

3 a) One in every four persons in Eastbourne is retired. Give two reasons why a retired person might not welcome large numbers of tourists. (4 marks)
  b) Describe the attractions of a resort such as Eastbourne for a summer visitor. (4 marks)
4 a) Name two towns from which people might make a day trip to the Brecon Beacons National Park. (2 marks)
  b) Briefly explain how each of the following people might find recreational facilities to attract them in the Brecon Beacons: (i) a family with young children (ii) a person keen on outdoor pursuits. (4 marks)

TOTAL: 75 marks

Details for pupil profile sheet Unit 9

Knowledge and understanding

1 Unemployment
2 Choropleth map
3 Post-industrial stage of economic development
4 Government regional policy
5 Development Area, Intermediate Area
6 Enterprise Zone, Free Port
7 European Regional Development Fund
8 Leisure industry
9 Tourist honeypot
10 National Park, AONB, Country Park, SSSI

Skills

1 Draw a choropleth map
2 Interpret a choropleth map
3 Keep a daily record of leisure time for a week
4 Interpret statistical information from a table
5 Naming cities on an outline map, using an atlas
6 Draw a pie chart
7 Using a range of techniques to prepare a brochure
8 Depict information in a simple map and diagram
9 Role play
10 Decision-making

Values

1 An awareness of the natural environment
2 An awareness of the pressures of tourism
3 The significance of the values of those who make decisions about the mangement of the environment

Index

A
Aerospace 65
Africa, North 38
Africa, West 30, 36
Agri-business 18
Agricultural system 4, 7, 8
AONB (Areas of Outstanding Natural Beauty) 119
Appropriate Technology 99
Arable farming 8
Asia, South-East 40, 94, 100
Automation 63

B
Biotechnology 66
Brazil 92
Brecon Beacons 14, 74, 120
Business Parks 68, 106

C
Cambridge Science Park 66
Cash crops 34, 36
Chocolate 36, 46
Coal 74, 76
Cocoa 36, 46
Coffee 42
Common Agricultural Policy 26
Contract farming 7, 19
Co-operative farming 21
Cotton 39
Country Parks 119

D
Dagenham 51
Damodar Basin, India 90
Denmark: farming 20

E
East Anglia: farming 6, 18
           industry 66
Economic rent 11
El Eijido, Spain 23
Enterprise Zone 84, 113
European Community 15, 23, 26, 114
ECSC (European Coal and Steel Community) 115
EIB (European Investment Bank) 115
ERDF (European Regional Development Fund) 114
ESF (European Social Fund) 115
Extensive farming 8

F
Factory farming 24
Fjordside farming 16
'Food mountains' 26
Ford Europe 51, 60
Fulani people 30

G
Ganges Basin, India 32
Gateshead 71
Gezira, Sudan 38
Ghana: farming 36
Greenfield site 66
Green Revolution 33, 40

H
Hedge clearance 18
Heritage Coast 119
Hill farming 14
Hypermarket 71

I
India 32, 90
Industrial system 44
Integrated iron and steel works 57
Intensive farming 8, 24
Iron and steel industry 56, 58, 72, 74, 76, 90
Irrigation 22
Ivory Coast 36

J

K
Korea, North 96
Korea, South 96

L
Lake District 6
Liverpool 51
Lomé Convention 27
London 68, 84
London Docklands Development Corporation 84

M
Malaysia: farming 34
Manchester 50, 68, 70
Milford Haven 55
Motor vehicle industry 50, 60, 62, 92
Multi-national company 46, 89
Multiplier effect 49

N
National Parks 118, 120
National Scenic Areas 118
Netherlands 78, 80
Newport 86
NICs (Newly Industrialised Countries) 94
Nigeria 30
Nile Basin 38
Norway: farming 16

O
Oil refining 54, 78
Oxford 62

P
Pastoral farming 8
Plantation farming 34
Port Talbot 58

Q

R
Randstad 80
Reading 83
Rice farming 32, 40
Robotics 63
Rotterdam 78, 87
Rover Group 63
Rubber 34

S
Savanna climate 30
Science Parks 66
Shipbuilding 64
Singapore 100
SSSI (Sites of Special Scientific Interest) 119
Spain: farming 22
       vehicle industry 51
Standard Man Days (SMD) 10
Subsistence farming 8, 32
Sudan 38
Swindon 102, 104, 106, 108
System 4

T
Transhumance 17

U
Unemployment 110

V
Von Thunen model of agricultural land use 10

W
Wales 14, 54, 58, 74, 76, 86, 87, 120
Wealth creation 46
Weber's theory of industrial location 48
Western Corridor 66, 83, 104

Acknowledgements

The publishers would like to thank the following for their permission to reproduce photographs:

Aerocamera-Bart Hofmeester p80; Aero-Schiphol p78; Airviews (M/C) Ltd. p68; Aspect pp8 (*both*), 30, 44 (*top right, bottom left and right*), 44 (*centre bottom*), 88 (*left*); Barnabys p34 (*bottom*); Brecon Beacons National Park pp20 (*top right*), 121 (*left*); British Aerospace p64 (*top left*); British Chicken Information Service p24 (*bottom*); Cadbury-Schweppes plc. pp37, 46; J. Allan Cash pp6 (*top*), 31, 116; John Cornwell p76 (*both*); Daily Telegraph Colour Library p5 (*bottom*); Dan-Yr-Ogof Caves p120 (*top left*); Patrick Eagar p44 (*top left*); Embraer S/A p88 (*right*); Firo-Foto pp22, 23; Fokker p81; Food and Agriculture Organization pp38, 40; Foods from Spain p5 (*top left*); Ford Motor Company Ltd. pp50 (*both*), 51 (*both*), 60, 115; Ford Brazil S/A p92 (*both*); Paul Francis Photography p 71 (*bottom*); Richard and Sally Greenhill p111; Handford Photography p84 (*right*); Hewlett Packard p82 (*bottom left*); Jimmy Holmes p5 (*top right*); Chris Honeywell pp20, 36; Hutchison Library pp5 (*centre*), 11, 17 (*left*), 34 (*top*), 41, 45 (*top*), 94, 96; Rob Judges pp71 (*top*), 106 (*both*); LDDC pp84 (*centre*), 85; Michael Manni p67, (*top*); Massey Ferguson pp6 (*top*), 18, 19; Mittet Foto p17 (*right*); MOD/MARS pp64 (*top right, bottom left and right*), 65; Museum in Docklands Project p84 (*left*); Napp Laboratories p67 (*bottom*); Nigel Press Associates Ltd p39; Neil Punnett pp14 (*both*), 70 (*both*), 120 (*bottom*), 121 (*left*); Youth Hostels Association p119; J. Sainsbury plc p4; Sealand Aerial Photography p82 (*top right*); Arthur Shepherd pp6 (*bottom*), 9 (*both*), 24 (*top centre*), 27; South American Pictures p93 (*both*); Steel Times p91 (*both*); Jeffrey Tabberner p82 (*top left and bottom right*); Borough of Thamesdown pp103, 104; Topham p26; West Air pp55, 59, 66, 77, 118; Wonderworld plc p117.

The illustrations are by Richard Hook, Vanessa Luff, and Oxford Illustrators.

Cover photograph by Dennis Gilbert.

Oxford University Press, Walton Street, Oxford OX2 6DP

Oxford New York Toronto
Delhi Bombay Calcutta Madras Karachi
Kuala Lumpur Singapore Hong Kong Tokyo
Nairobi Dar es Salaam Cape Town
Melbourne Auckland Madrid

and associated companies in
Berlin Ibadan

Oxford is a trade mark of Oxford University Press

© Oxford University Press 1989
First published 1989
Reprinted 1992

ISBN 0 19 913325 5

All rights reserved. No part of this publication may be reproduced, stored in a retrieval system, or transmitted, in any form or by any means, without the prior permission in writing of Oxford University Press. Within the UK, exceptions are allowed in respect of any fair dealing for the purpose of research or private study, or criticism or review, as permitted under the Copyright, Designs and Patents Act, 1988, or in the case of reprographic reproduction in accordance with the terms of licences issued by the Copyright Licensing Agency. Enquiries concerning reproduction outside those terms and in other countries should be sent to the Rights Department, Oxford University Press, at the address above.

Set by Tradespools Ltd., Frome, Somerset
Printed in Hong Kong

Pupil Profile Sheet
Agriculture and Industry

Unit ☐

Pupil name _____

After completing this unit you should be able to do the following:

KNOWLEDGE AND UNDERSTANDING	YES	NO

Understand and use the following terms and concepts:

1. _____
2. _____
3. _____
4. _____
5. _____
6. _____
7. _____
8. _____
9. _____
10. _____

SKILLS
Understand and use the following skills:

1. _____
2. _____
3. _____
4. _____
5. _____
6. _____
7. _____
8. _____
9. _____
10. _____

VALUES

1. _____
2. _____
3. _____